The
HEART of the HOME

The
HEART of the HOME

To young wives and mothers
a handbook for the home

The most important part of the Lord's work you will ever do, will be the work you do within the walls of your own home, and for the family He has given you.

Harold B. Lethem

Cheryl Erwin Eldridge

Xulon Press

Xulon Press Elite
555 Winderley Pl, Suite 225
Maitland, FL 32751
407.339.4217
www.xulonpress.com

© 2023 by Cheryl Erwin Eldridge

All rights reserved solely by the author. The author guarantees all contents are original and do not infringe upon the legal rights of any other person or work. No part of this book may be reproduced in any form without the permission of the author.

Due to the changing nature of the Internet, if there are any web addresses, links, or URLs included in this manuscript, these may have been altered and may no longer be accessible. The views and opinions shared in this book belong solely to the author and do not necessarily reflect those of the publisher. The publisher therefore disclaims responsibility for the views or opinions expressed within the work.

Unless otherwise indicated, Scripture quotations taken from the Holy Bible, New International Version (NIV). Copyright © 1973, 1978, 1984, 2011 by Biblica, Inc.™. Used by permission. All rights reserved.

Scripture quotations taken from the King James Version (KJV)–public domain.

Paperback ISBN-13: 978-1-66288-979-0
Ebook ISBN-13: 978-1-66288-980-6

Dedication

I would like to dedicate this book to my dear husband and best friend, Bill, who has encouraged me every step along this path and without whom this book would have never been written.

And

To my two dear mothers, my mother Geraldine Erwin and my mother-in-law Pearl Eldridge, who were both shining examples of a woman dedicated to God and her family, who personified the true, Heart of the Home.

Introduction

By faith Noah, when warned about things not yet seen, in holy fear built an ark to save his family.
Hebrews 11:7

Dear reader,

For many years I have felt a longing in my heart to pass on the homemaking knowledge I have learned in my fifty-plus years as a wife and mother, to teach young women the skills they need to first and foremost be strong women of God but also to be the real heart of the home— women who would be good helpmates to their husbands, kind and loving wives, caring for their husbands, creating a home they would be glad to come home to, who would be a good and godly example to their families and friends.

These would be women who would train their children using not only the stories of the Bible but more importantly, the truths and wisdom of the Bible. These women would also train their children to have integrity in all they do, to be self-reliant, responsible, and honorable people. They would be kind and loving as they train their children, patient with little ones and wise with teenagers.

At one time or another, we all need someone to come along and help us in life. I've had many women help me along the way, some through just a shining example that I wanted to be like, others gave me practical advice that helped immensely. Whether you are a young woman just starting this wonderful journey of being a wife and mother or a woman who has been such for a long time but just can't seem to get control over it all, I would like to share with you what has taken me a lifetime of being a wife and mother myself to learn. One thing I know for sure is that this is the most important job we will ever have. Its influence will last far beyond your lifetime into many generations yet to come.

I've studied a lot of different methods women use in their homemaking skills that are truly incredible, many of them I wish I had known when my children were young—it would have made life much easier for all of us.

I've seen the feminist movement destroying one home after another. It is a strong force in our world today and is portrayed everywhere you look. Women take the lead role, often leaving the husband to wonder if he is anything more than a paycheck or just another pair of hands to get the work done. In commercials men are often portrayed as inept; the woman is the one with all the answers, and she takes over his role as leader of the family, and to avoid an argument he just stays quiet.

What a sad state our nation has fallen to today. For the sake of our families, we need to revisit some of the old ways, some of the ways of our mothers and grandmothers. Maybe their way wasn't 100 percent right, but I believe homes were a lot happier and children grew up with more of a sense of security, feeling that they were an important part of the family unit. Today so many dads have their own life, moms have theirs, and children have theirs, all disconnected from each other. Then we wonder why the divorce rate is so high, even among Christian homes, and why children have no respect for authority. My heart breaks as I see the number of young couples that are so unhappy in their marriage relationship, each one blaming the other for the problems that arise, with no one taking responsibility for their own actions. We all need to be on our faces before God and get some direction and insight, as to how the home should be run, what each person's role is, and how to carry out those roles for the honor of God and for the saving of our families.

Becoming godly women and building a godly home does not happen by accident; it takes a lot of planning and work to carry out those plans. Always remember there is an enemy that is constantly working to turn husbands and wives against each other and children and parents against each other. He is very subtle and works on each member of the family, whispering lies in their ear that will cause separation. Once he has us thinking the other one is against us and they are the one at fault, it is easier for him to break up the home or at least leave its people powerless to help each other, keeping us from growing spiritually together as a strong Christian family.

Proverbs 24: 30-34 gives us insight into how easy it is to lose our families without even trying:

I went past the field of a sluggard, past the vineyard of someone who has no sense;
thorns had come up everywhere, the ground was covered with weeds, and the
stone wall was in ruins. I applied my heart to what I observed and learned a lesson
from what I saw: A little sleep, a little slumber, a little folding of the hands to
rest—and poverty will come on you like a thief and scarcity like an armed man.

Proverbs 1:5 also tells us, *Let the wise listen and add to their learning, and let the discerning get guidance.*

Knowledge is useless unless it is used.

The wise are always watching and listening to others. They sift through the information they have found and keep the good and discard the rest. If we find knowledge and don't use it, it is useless to us. Once we find what to do in a certain situation, it's up to us to do it. We must constantly be on guard for the well-being of our family. Yes, it will take a lot of effort, but it will pay big dividends as we live in a home full of happiness and peace. We'll see our marriages and children do more than just survive; they will thrive.

Proverbs 1: 20-21 says, *Out in the open wisdom calls aloud, she raises her voice in the public square; on top of the wall she cries out, at the city gate she makes her speech.*

This means we should look around and take notice of what other wives and mothers have done and what results they have gotten, then follow the example of those who have done well and avoid the mistakes others have made. When you need advice, get it from those who have been where you are and have made the right, sometimes hard or unpopular decisions to get through it, and have gotten good results. Those who are in the same situation in life that you are in can't give you good advice because they don't even know what to do themselves. It's up to you to find and follow the right map made by those who have succeeded at what you want to succeed at.

Acts 20:28 cautions us, *Keep watch over yourselves and all the flock* [your circle of influence] *of which the Holy Spirit has made you overseers.*

I believe wives and mothers everywhere desire to be good and nurturing caregivers to their families. But how do we do that in a world that indoctrinates us to believe the only person to care about is our own self, that the only opinion that counts is our opinion, that our self-worth is only validated by our careers? The family unit will be the major loser. As we see this in the world around us, we must ask ourselves two very important questions. Do we want our precious families to be one of the losers or do we want our family unit to be secure and strong, a place where those we love most will grow strong spiritually and morally. Yes, indeed, that is exactly what we want!

With men and women both working, it gives each one an idea of what the other one deals with. The wife understands why the husband needs a place of peace to unwind after dealing with people and pressure all day, because when she comes home from work, she needs it too. And the husband understands all the work the wife does to keep the house running smoothly and dealing with the children because he works alongside her to get everything done.

As mothers it's important to take seriously the important task the Lord has entrusted us with; the task of training our children to follow Christ. Most of the great ministers, past and present, have had mothers that have consistently and diligently taught their children the Word of God.

On January 28, 1852, Windell Phillips said about our country's freedom and wellbeing that "Eternal vigilance is the price of liberty." The same is true of our homes and families. It may be easier to let everyone have their own way with no clear and defined direction or rules, but it will be the downfall of our home and family. We'll either look back at years well spent, or we'll look back with regret at the years we've wasted. This choice is up to us. To get good results we must, purposefully make the decision to do whatever is necessary, and we have to keep making those same decisions every day.

When the day's work is done and you sit down with your husband and children around you, knowing you're doing all you can for each member of your precious family, you will see that your children are following the Lord, and respecting their dad, you, and themselves. What greater gift can a woman have?

I read once that the reason women have more fat cells than men is because men are the ones who go out and do the hard work to take care of and protect their families, so they need more muscle. Women are the nurturers, the ones who cuddle and comfort the children. We are in a way, the cushion for them from the hardness and callousness of the world. Yes, indeed ladies, we are the true heart of the home.

Because of its numerous topics, you most likely won't read this book straight through like a novel. It is more like a handbook covering the many phases of our life, of our family's life, and of our home.

You will find that I use a lot of scripture references, sometimes the same scripture in different places depending on how they fit the different subjects. The reason for this is that I want to tell you more than my opinion or my way of looking at these areas in life. I want you to see what the Bible says. God's opinion and direction is by far more important than my own. For the Bible is our go-to book for every area of our life. It is God's gift to us to show us how to have the best life we can have a life of peace and joy, a life that will not only bless and bring peace to us but also to our precious families. After all, we are the number one helper and encourager to our husband, and we are the number one teacher to our children. We really do set the atmosphere in our homes. A home of peace and joy can only be created by following God with our whole hearts. His Word instructs us how to achieve a home that will nurture our children and help them find the best path in life that will ultimately lead them to a life of peace of heart and mind as they become adults and have a home of their own.

Unless otherwise noted all scriptures are taken from the New International Version.

Table of Contents

Chapter 1
The Lady of the House 1
Chapter 2
The Man of the House. 43
Chapter 3
The Children of the House 75
Chapter 4
The Guests of the House. 144
Chapter 5
The House. 154

Chapter 1

The Women of the House

*Draw nigh to God,
and he will draw nigh to you.*
James 4:8

Getting to Know Our Heavenly Father

In the first part of this first chapter we're going to begin by talking about the importance of our relationship with God because our relationship with God will greatly affect every other relationship in our life. We will also be talking about how to grow in that relationship.

With any relationship that is important to us, time is the most important thing we can invest in it. So naturally, the more time we spend with God, the closer we will be to Him. Our Heavenly Father is just waiting for us to take the first step toward Him, then He will be right there to meet us. Let's take a look at James 4:8. Here we'll see that God himself tells us how to have a close relationship with

Him. He says, if you will, *Come near to God and he will come near to you.* When I think about the Scripture we just read, I can see a loving father crouched down with his arms stretched out, coaxing a little toddler who is just learning to walk to come to him. Our Heavenly Father will draw us to Him, but then it is up to us to take the necessary steps to read our Bible and pray; this will bring us closer to God. We must be diligent to make sure we spend quality time with God.

The Bible is the greatest instruction book ever written. There are many instruction books for life. There are instruction books for everything from our dishwasher to our car. We read instruction books on losing weight, dressing for success, or even how to apply our makeup. There are probably untold millions of instruction books to advise us. These can be helpful in some areas of our life, telling us how to do some of the natural things, but the Bible will teach us not only some of the natural things in life, but most importantly it will teach us all the spiritual things. If we read it and obey what it says, we will have an awesome life here, and, one day, an eternal home in Heaven. The Bible is assuredly the greatest instruction book of all time. There is more wisdom in it than in any other book ever written, and since it is Holy Spirit inspired, it is straight from our Heavenly Father's heart. Who better to get advice from?

If we take what the Bible tells us to do, or not do, and think seriously about what the result would be to each action, we will find that God only tells us these things to show us how to have a happy, peaceful, and successful life. God's laws are not to keep us from enjoying life; they are made out of His love for us, to protect us from the bad and hurtful things in life. If we follow them, we will avoid many heartaches and tears.

Devotion Time

Make a habit of daily devotions and prayer. 2 Peter 3:18 instructs us to, *grow in the grace and knowledge of our Lord and Savior Jesus Christ*. Growing in grace and knowledge only comes from reading and meditating on the words of the Bible and time spent in prayer. If we are really serious about wanting to know God, we must read and study His Word. This will take some time and dedication on our part, but we will receive many benefits, not only for us but for our families as well. In it we will find many examples of how God helped people in the past and what pleases Him and what doesn't.

Read with the desire to learn.

It's important to remember that when we read our Bible that quality is the important thing, not quantity. If we diligently read and then meditate on what we have read in a portion of scripture, we are more likely to understand what our Heavenly Father is saying to us through those words. Ask yourself, "What can I glean from this portion of scripture? How do these scriptures apply to my life?"

In my early years of seriously following the Lord, I learned that He doesn't talk to us with a great thundering voice. The main way that He speaks to us is though His

Word. I soon learned that page after page of His Word was filled with Him speaking to me.

Keeping a journal to write down any scripture that stands out to you will help you tremendously. In your own words, write what you understand those scriptures are saying to you. Then see how many things you can pull out of them that you hadn't noticed before.

Meditating on God's Word is an extremely important thing to do. Let's take a look at how we do this. For example, we'll take the familiar scripture of John 3:16: *For God so loved the world that he gave his one and only Son, that whoever believes in him shall not perish but have eternal life.* Now let's take a closer look at each phrase.

For God so loved: He *so* loved. This was not just a little bit of love; this was a depth of love that we can't even imagine.

That he gave his one and only Son Wow, that is some kind of love! Could I do that, could you do that? Could we give our only son knowing what he would be going through to pay the price for the sins of the whole world? That had a big price tag on it! Here our Heavenly Father says that He loved us so much that He was willing to give the most precious gift that He has, to pay the price for the sins that we committed.

That whoever: Let's think about that: whosoever. That means from the king in his palace to the poorest man living on the streets, from the person who always does the right and honorable thing, to the one who always does the wrong thing, caring not who it hurts.

Believes in him: That is all we have to do, believe in Him.

Shall not perish but have eternal life: This means that with God there are only two ways to go at the end of our lives. One way is to go to Heaven. 1 Corinthians 2:9 tells us what is waiting for us in Heaven, *Eye hath not seen, nor ear heard, neither have entered into the heart of man, the things which God hath prepared for them that love him.* There are things so wonderful that we can't imagine in our wildest dreams.

The other ways is to go to Hell. When the Bible speaks of perishing, it doesn't mean that at the end of their life a person, ever so gently goes to sleep forever. People say, "Oh it won't be so bad. All my friends will be there to party with me," but that's not what the Bible says. If a person goes to hell, Matthew 22:13 (KJV) tells us what is waiting for them there, *There will be weeping and gnashing of teeth.* In fact, it will be terrible beyond our wildest dreams.

Meditating on God's Word will not only help you remember what you've read, but you will most likely be surprised by the way God will speak to your heart by doing this. There may be a problem that you're dealing with that these scriptures will guide you in knowing what to do or just a question that you've been wondering about that these very scriptures will reveal the answer to. I have found that if I am having trouble understanding what the scripture says, I can ask the Holy Spirit to help me understand it. Then I meditate on the scripture and read it over and over a few times until I get a clear understanding of what it really means. Sometimes the understanding comes right away, sometimes it takes a little bit longer, but if we keep our spiritual ears and eyes open, it will always come.

*Reflect on what I am saying
for the Lord will give you insight into all this.*
2 Timothy 2:7

Luke tells us that when Jesus' disciples were having a hard time understanding the scriptures. *He opened their minds so they could understand the Scriptures* (Luke 24:45). This is a prayer I often pray before I begin reading my Bible: "Lord I want to hear from You. I pray that You will open my mind like You did Your disciples so that I will understand Your Word."

God's Guidance

God is always right there with us to help us with any problem we may have. His Word is His promises. We can count on them and claim them when we need them. When we find a promise that covers the problem we have, we'll often find that it has two parts. The first part is something for us to do, and when we do what God instructs us to do, we can count on Him to do what He has promised He will do. Philippians 4:6-7 are two-part scriptures that show us how this works. The first part of it is ours: *Do not be anxious about anything*. There are times that this is very hard to do. We have to, on purpose, rein in our thoughts. There may be times when our mind is going wild with the "what if" thoughts. What if this happens, or what if that happens? The rest of our part is *In every situation, by prayer* [worshiping, fellowshipping with God] *and petition,* [making requests] *with thanksgiving* [giving thanks for what he's already done] *present your requests to God.* This tells us that when we make our requests to God, we should also start thanking Him for the times He has come through for us in the past and turned other difficult situations around. Remembering these other answered prayers will make our faith grow, and once again our hearts will overflow with thankfulness and confidence that God will answer this prayer just like He did the others. Once we do these things, which are our part, then we can count on God to do His part, which is *And the peace of God, which transcends all understanding,* [you will not understand why you have peace, neither will anyone else understand it] *will guard your hearts and your minds in Christ Jesus* [picture a soldier with a shield and sword standing guard between you and the problem]."

Many years ago, when my husband Bill, was only fifty-three years old, he had a double aortic aneurysm on his heart. You can imagine how my mind was bombarded with the "what if" thoughts. He went through a horrible eleven-hour surgery, but while he was in surgery I was enveloped with an unwavering sense of peace that he would survive. The days that followed were very hard and could have gone either way, but that overwhelming peace remained. Oh there were times that were very scary, where my peace would waver, but this was where I truly learned, without a doubt, the true meaning of this promise because I had, *the peace of God, which transcends all understanding* guarding my heart and my mind. There was no reason in the world for me to have peace that he would survive. Some of the things the doctor told us could happen after this surgery didn't even register on my mind, for the Lord was standing guard between me and the spirit of fear. It wasn't until it was all over, and Bill was well on the road to recovery, that I was told and then remembered, some of the things that the doctor had said about his chance of survival. A couple of days after his surgery, I saw a picture of something that has been indelibly engraved on my mind. It was a picture of one of his doctors that had come into his room to examine him. After he had finished the examination, he leaned up against the wall, crossed his arms, and looked intently at Bill. Then with a voice of someone who could hardly believe what he was seeing, he said, "Bill, it's only because of God that you're still here." He had seen, with his own eyes, what condition my husband's heart was in, and what had to be done to repair it. Thankfully, Bill had a full recovery, and he is strong and healthy today. Are we thankful? Yes, indeed, we are beyond thankful.

When we read our Bible, we are planting the promises that God has given us in our heart and mind. Then when we need them, the Holy Spirit will bring those promises back to us. For instance, when we are feeling fearful and all alone, the Holy Spirit will remind us of this promise from God. *Do not fear, for I am with you, do not be dismayed, for I am your God. I will strengthen you and help you; I will uphold you with my righteous right hand* (Isiah 41:10).

When we tell our children that we're going to get them some ice cream in a little while, in their innocence and simplicity they don't have a doubt in their mind that we will do what we said we would do even though they don't see the ice cream right then. This is how completely our

Heavenly Father wants us to believe what He tells us in His Word. His Word is His will. In it we will find many scriptures that give us important instructions that show us how we can have a good life and how to avoid the pitfalls the enemy has planned to trip us up. The enemy of our soul knows exactly what temptations will work on each one of us. This temptation may not be sinful, it may be just a distraction to keep us away from pursuing God. The devil's goal is to get us to take just one little step off God's chosen path. Then he'll tempt us to take just one more, little by little hoping to get us completely off God's chosen path. When we get a bit discouraged, feeling down, or just plain overtired, he makes sure that temptation is right there waiting for us, because he knows that it's easier to get us when our guard is down, even just a little. What he's really after is to get us to step off the path that God has chosen for us and get us on the path of destruction that he has chosen for us.

That's when we must put what we read in God's Word into practice so that it will help us grow spiritually. Like James 1:22 instructs us, *Do not merely listen to the word, and so deceive yourselves. Do what it says.*

Pray about Everything

Like we need sleep and rest to rejuvenate our bodies, we need time spent with God to rejuvenate our spirit. I find the time that I give God my undivided attention, praying in private, and putting my whole focus on Him alone, really gives me a special sense of closeness to Him. That's when I can really talk to Him and unburden my heart.

It is good to keep a pen and paper handy when we're spending time with God in prayer because that's when He will often reveal some important information to us. He may give us a thought that will help us with something that we are endeavoring to do, or an answer to a problem we have. If we write down what God has impressed on our heart we will remember it. This also shows Him that we value what He has told us, and that we don't want to forget what He has impressed on our heart. If we don't write down what God tells us we are more likely to forget what He has said and then when we need those very words for encouragement or direction, they will be forgotten.

If we just pray general prayers when we pray for others like, "God bless so and so," it doesn't give God much direction to work with. But if we can find out exactly what that person needs and pray specifically for that need, we will find that we have more power in our prayers. My husband is a hunter and that is where I got the image of "Pinpoint Prayer," that I'd like to share with you here. This is how it works. If I was target practicing and I used a shotgun with fine-shot, I would spray the target with little bits of fine-shot, I may hit the bullseye and I may not. Even if I do, it will only be with tiny scattered holes. But if I use a rifle with a strong scope, loaded with a bullet which has one large piece of lead, I will, without fail hit the bullseye every time. That's exactly what we need to do with our prayers. If possible, find out exactly what the need is, and then pray specifically for that need. If we do this, we will find that our prayers are much more effective.

> *The prayer of a righteous person is powerful and effective.*
> James 5:16

1Thessalonians 5:17 tells us to, *Pray continually*. We can also keep a prayer on our lips as we go about our day. We may hear of someone who is ill or has some kind of problem that they need prayer for, and we can say a prayer for them right then. It's always better to pray as soon as we hear a need, that way we don't have to worry that we may forget to pray for it later. It's also good to keep a special notebook to write down prayer requests. There we can record the person's name, a short explanation of their need, and the date. Then don't forget to make a note of thanks to God when the prayer is answered.

As you go about your day, ask God to help you in all you do. If it's important to you, it's important to your heavenly Father. When you start cooking a meal, pray that it will nourish and strengthen your family, and that they will enjoy it. When you go shopping, pray that you will get a close parking place and that as you shop, you will spend your money wisely. Pray that what you buy will be something that you will be pleased with, how many times do we purchase a piece of clothing that looks good only to wash it once or twice and have the seams go crooked? You get the idea, let God guide you throughout your day. It's important to keep the line of communication open between us and our Heavenly Father.

Therefore I tell you, whatever you ask for in prayer,
believe that you have received it,
and it will be yours.
Mark 11:24

Making Decisions

The first thing to do when we have a decision to make, is to talk to God and ask Him to give us His direction for this situation.

Your word is a lamp for my feet,
a light on my path.
Psalm 119:105

If we sincerely seek God's advice, He will guide our thoughts and desires in the way that we should go. God also answers by a still, small voice that comes from deep within our heart. Other times He may lead us to something in His Word, or even in a book or devotional that will be the perfect answer to what we are looking for. Not only will this be the direction that's pleasing to Him, but it will also be the best direction for us. One direction may look like the best to us, but God knows if that direction could lead us into some danger that we don't see. God always wants to guide our steps around any danger we may be headed for on our own.

When we feel like we have no clear answer and we're not sure of which direction to take, that is when we should just stay still and wait for God to answer us. He will give us guidance in His time, and it will always be the right direction at the right time. Waiting is the hardest part because we think we should be doing something. But be assured that God is working out all the details. Sometimes that means that we have to wait until other things are lined up that we know nothing about, but if we are willing to wait for His timing, we'll find out that everything will work out just right, and we'll be thankful that we waited for His answer.

Quite often, God only tells us the first few steps to take in the direction He wants us to go. Once we take these few steps, He will give us more directions, sometimes just a little at a time. But remember, God doesn't get in a hurry, and you may have to wait a bit until you get the next step that God wants you to take. Think about each choice and see which one gives you peace. You'll have a prickly, uneasy feeling if things aren't right. Always follow what brings peace to your heart. God will give you peace when you find the direction He wants you to take. Remember what we're told in Psalm 34:14, *Seek peace and pursue it.*

Here is an example from my own life that will illustrate what we are talking about. When I was getting ready to retire, we were all prepared to move to another city. We bought the house and had most of our furniture and belongings moved in, keeping just the essentials.

But there seemed to be no buyers for the house we were in and wanted to sell. Month after month went by with nothing happening and the time for my retirement was getting closer and closer. We just couldn't understand what the hold- up was, and we were so sure that this move was God's will for us. We wondered, "Did we miss hearing the will of God?" Then, just a couple of weeks before my retirement date was reached, we got an offer on our house which was even more than we had asked for. When it was all said and done, we looked back and saw the hand of God so clearly. If our house would have sold while I was still working, we would have had to move into an apartment, which would have cost us quite a bit of extra money, and the owners would have most likely wanted a year's lease. So we were spared the expense of an apartment that we only needed for a short time. How blessed we were to be able to stay in our own home right up to my retirement date. We even ended up with an extra week to finish moving out. Now we could easily see that the Lord was looking out for us all along and doing what was best for us. But before we were able to sell the house there were times when it was very hard to, by faith, wait on God's timing.

Now let's take a look at the five blessings we received because even though we didn't understand, we still followed God's lead.

1. We sold our house at just the right time.
2. We received more money for it than we had asked.
3. We were spared the expense of an apartment.

4. We were able to stay in our own home all the way up to my retirement date.
5. We even ended up with an extra week after I retired to finish moving out.

A word of caution:

There may be times when someone may speak a word of direction to you that they say is from God. Always remember that when God wants you to know something, He will speak to your heart *before* He tells anyone else. Someone else may confirm what He has already said to you, but be very cautious of those who tell you that God has told them to tell you a direction for your life that He has not already spoken to you about. God doesn't work that way.

Choosing our Friends

> *The righteous choose their friends carefully.*
> Proverbs 12:26

Choosing our friends is a very important part of our lives. Notice that I said *choosing*. We must purposefully, and most of all prayerfully, choose our friends. This is something we have to be very careful about because the right friends will make a lasting influence on our lives, as will the wrong ones. We may think that someone seems like they are a wonderful person, that they are kind and loving, only to find out later that they are deceitful, critical, and manipulative. Seek God for His direction, He knows each person's heart. *The Lord does not look at the things people look at. People look at the outward appearance, but the Lord looks at the heart* (1 Samuel 16:7).

The influence of the people we surround ourselves with will eventually either raise or lower our standards. They will either help us become the best version of ourselves or pull us down to a lesser version of ourselves. We all need people in our lives who help us rise to our full potential and challenge us to become what God has called us to be.

Walk with the wise and become wise.
Proverbs 13:20

An important thing to remember is that we will become like the people we associate with, so we must be diligent to surround ourselves with people we want to be like. We must find good and godly friends, those who desire to walk with the Lord like we do. They will be faithful prayer partners, and we will be able to help each other when one of us has a need.

Diligently look for friends that have the same high moral standards, values, and goals that you have. When you find someone like this, work intently to cultivate a close friendship with them. Most likely, your children will become close friends with their children. Knowing this, we must be extremely careful in choosing friends. We must think long and hard about what kind of example they will set for our children because our children are not only watching us, they will be watching our friends too. Building lasting friendships with godly friends will not only help you but will greatly help your children too. If they see you choose your friends wisely, and you talk to them about the importance of it, they will be more likely to do the same.

We had a family member who had successfully fought and broke the habit of smoking, which was very hard for him. Then, one day he saw a Christian man from our small church smoking and he decided, "if it's ok for him to smoke, then it's ok for me." With that, he started smoking again and smoked for the rest of his life. Sadly he died at fifty-three with heart disease. I can't say that it was the other person's fault, but their influence did not help him, it hurt him and opened the door to the wrong path.

Taking Care of Ourselves

It's hard to do a good job of taking care of our family if we don't take care of ourselves. When we get overtired and drained, it's the perfect time for Satan to plant some seeds of bitterness and resentment into our mind. He will whisper in our ear something like, "You have to do everything," and, "No one works as hard as you do and what thanks do you get?"

If you constantly give out without replenishing yourself, pretty soon you'll have nothing left to give. It's important to take some time just for yourself, to do some things you enjoy. If you keep a calendar of appointments and things to do, schedule yourself a block of time, and then do what you can to keep it. Everyone has something they like to do that helps them relax and recharge their batteries. You'll go back to your family refreshed and with a great attitude. You'll be doing your family a favor if you take care of yourself.

Read good books that encourage you and teach you how to live a life that pleases God. Also read books on subjects that interest you and those that teach you how to deal with any difficulties you may be facing. Many people have been in the same situation that you are in and have written information on how to successfully deal with that specific problem. But always be careful to make sure their teaching lines up with the Word of God.

Our Conduct

Have integrity.

> *The integrity of the upright guides them.*
> Proverbs 11:3

We want our children to have integrity in every area of their life, so we must also have integrity in ours. No matter how old they are, they are watching us, and they learn by example, mostly our example. This is an awesome responsibility.

Stand up for what is right.

> *She is clothed with strength and dignity.*
> Proverbs 31:25

To walk honorably shows others what a real Christ follower does in every circumstance in life.

We must have the strength to stand for what's right whether it is popular or not. There may be times we have to stand alone when we stand for what's right, but we are never really alone, because as the apostle Paul said so many years ago, *At my first defense, no one came to my support, but everyone deserted me. May it not be held against them. But the Lord stood at my side and gave me strength* (2Timothy 4:16-17). So we must always remember that the Lord is right there with us, all the time, for He promises us, *Never will I leave you; never will I forsake you.* (Hebrews 13:5).

Don't gossip.

> *Slander no one, be peaceable and considerate,*
> *and always be gentle toward everyone.*
> Titus 3:2

If we hear some unkind gossip being said about another person, we should keep it to ourselves unless it is something that honestly needs to be told to a certain person, and then only told to that specific person that it will affect. If we pass on what we've heard to other people, it will poison their thoughts and actions toward the gossiped person. We very seldom know all the circumstances and we may have even heard the story wrong ourselves. So often we don't know what has caused this other person to act the way they did. We only see the result of what has happened to them in life that has produced the actions that are hurting others or themselves. When we hear gossip, we should take it to the Lord in prayer. Isn't that what we would like others to do for us if we did something wrong? When you start to say something and you feel a check in your spirit, just that uneasy feeling, stop right there because that's how God is telling you not to say what is on your mind.

Clean up after yourself.

In a restaurant, dirty dishes are expected, but if we or our children make a mess on the table, we should always clean it up. If our little one has dropped what they were eating on the floor, ask the waiter to bring a broom, and offer to clean up what was dropped. Most likely they will do it for us, but it is only common courtesy to at least offer.

When you are in the ladies' room washing your hands and water splatters around the sink, always wipe it up. If you drop something, pick it up and put it where it belongs. But never pick up what someone else has dropped. They may have been sick, and you don't want to take a chance on catching any sickness that they may have.

In all we do, we must do our best to have a spirit of excellence. This doesn't mean that what we do is always perfect, but it does mean that we always do the best that we know how.

Our Circle of Influence

> *Be shepherds of God's flock that is under your care, watching over them, not because you must, but because you are willing, as God wants you to be; being examples to the flock. And when the Chief Shepherd appears, you will receive the crown of glory that will never fade away.*
> 1Peter 5: 2-4

We have all been given a circle of influence. This consists of the people in our lives that our actions and our words influence one way or the other. Some people are given large circles, and some are given small circles, but no matter which we are given, it is our responsibility to deliberately use our words and deeds to influence those in our circle in a way that will set a good and godly example for them to follow. We must nurture and care for every person in that circle of ours. It is a very precious and important task.

> *Guard what has been entrusted to your care.*
> 1Timothy 6:20

There are four layers in our circle of influence. The first is our immediate family, which consists of our husband and children, they are at the very center of our circle, we should spend most of our time with them. They are given to us by God and are the most important people God wants us to influence by respecting and loving our husband and by diligently training our children, loving them, and leading them to God. In doing this we will be like Noah, building an ark for the saving of our household.

> *By faith Noah, when warned about things not yet seen,
> in holy fear built an ark to save his family*
> (Hebrews 11:7).

So many people say they love the Lord and want to work for Him, but they just don't know what He wants them to do. God has given us a very important assignment; taking care of our family and leading each one of them to God. Yes, we should do work in the church and do good things to help others when we have time, but the main and most important job that God has given us is to teach and train the family He has given us, to love and serve Him. It is great to win others to the Lord, but if we go out day after day to help others and leave our family home alone without our godly guidance, we are not listening to the voice of God, who tells us to take care of our own family first.

The second circle is our extended family, which includes our parents, siblings, and their families. We should spend some time should be spent here but not as much as on our own family.

The third layer of the circle is our church family and our friends. The fourth are those we work with, and our acquaintances and neighbors. A limited amount of time should be spent here, but they too are our mission field.

One thing to keep in mind about our circle of influence is that it is much greater than we may realize because the influence we have on those God has given us, also influences others. Like ripples in water that start when something is thrown into it, our influence can go far beyond those we directly touch. An example could be when we say something to our children who in turn say the same thing to their friend at school, and that friend will likely go home and tell their parents about it, and so on and so on. This makes us realize how very important it is to be the right influence and say and do the right things, things that will lift people up and bring them closer to God.

Helping Others

> *God created us to do good work*
> *and He has prepared in advance*
> *those particular good works for us to do.*
> Ephesians 2:10.

Every time I read this Scripture, I am amazed all over again with the thought that God has the path all set up that He wants me to walk in, and that He has strewn along this path, good works that are waiting for me to do them. Then it is up to me to recognize and do them.

"Someone is waiting on the other side of our obedience."

I once heard this said by a missionary, what a thought that someone, maybe someone we don't even know, is waiting for us to say or do something that God assigned for us to do that will, in one way or another, be just what they need, at just the right time, maybe even something that will change the direction of their life.

Pray for God's direction in helping those in need for He has handpicked those particular people for us to help. Jesus didn't help everyone all the time; sometimes it was just one person in a crowd of many.

1 Peter 5:2 says that we should have the attitude that helping others is something we *get to do*, not something we have to do. *Feed the flock of God which is among you, taking the oversight thereof, not by constraint, but willingly; not for filthy lucre, but of a ready mind;* This attitude is what is pleasing to God. We are all ministers in one way or another. According to dictionary.com, the word minister, used as a verb, is defined as one to give service, care, or aid; attend, as to wants or necessities. We must bring them the Good News that Jesus loves them. As Christians we should be known by the love we show to others, and for doing the right thing, even when it's hard or unpopular. Pleasing God is the number one thing we need to be focused on.

There are two scriptures that set forth the commission that God has given us. The first tells us the profession that He has appointed us to, *We are ambassadors for Christ* (2

Corinthians 5:20 KJV). The second is where our citizenship ultimately lies, *Our citizenship is in heaven* (Philippians 3:20).

Dictionary.com defines an ambassador as "an accredited diplomat of the highest rank, sent by one government, (in this case, that would be God's government) to represent it on a temporary mission." Although our citizenship is in Heaven, we have been deployed to earth on a Heavenly mission. We are Jesus' hands and feet here in this world. We have a job to do, which is bring the lost to Christ while there is still time, and also to help those in need.

If we just look around us and keep our eyes and ears open, we will find many opportunities to be Jesus' feet to go where there is a need and His hands to do what He wants to be done. If we find a need and we have the ability and resources to fill it, we must do so, and do it with a willing heart. A willing heart is extremely important to God. 2 Corinthians 9:7 says, *Each of you should give what you have decided in your heart to give, not reluctantly or under compulsion, for God loves a cheerful giver.* We may ask, what can I do? The simple answer is, do what you can. Ask God to lead you to the ones He has chosen for you to help or encourage, to be a light in your world, to be kind and considerate to everyone. Sometimes just a smile will brighten someone else's day. Smiles are contagious, and we have no idea what personal battles others are facing. But we can count on the fact that everyone is fighting some kind of battle. Just a bit of extra kindness may be what keeps someone from doing the very thing that they will regret later on.

Everywhere we go, everything we say, and everything we do we are representing Christ to a lost and dying world. We are the only impression that some people will ever get of Him. We need to be diligently living a life that shows others the love of God. He is not judgmental or condemning; He just shows love, and that is what we should be doing too. John 3:17 tells us, *God did not send his Son into the world to condemn the world, but to save the world through him.*

So often people are drawn to groups of people who don't know God because those people make them feel loved and accepted; they are given the feeling that they are an important part of the group. We as Christians should do the same thing, not that we embrace sin, but we should embrace the sinner. God will deal with the sin in their lives; we need to love sinners into the kingdom.

> *She opens her arms to the poor and extends her hands to the needy.*
> Proverbs 31:20

Mother Teresa became famous worldwide because she simply saw a need and did what she could to fill it. Always be compassionate to those less fortunate than you are.

When Jesus gathered his twelve disciples unto him and commissioned them to spread the gospel throughout the world, He ended with telling them that they would be rewarded for even the smallest act of kindness. He said, *If anyone gives even a cup of cold water to one of these little ones who is my disciple, truly I tell you, that person will certainly not lose their reward* (Matthew 10:42).

Let's take a look at the sixth chapter of John where this is demonstrated. We find here in verses 1 through 9 the account of a hungry crowd and a little boy with the only lunch, among so many. His lunch consisted of two small fish and five barley loaves. When the little boy realized that everyone was hungry and not just him, and he heard that there was nothing for them to eat, he willingly gave what he had to Jesus. When Jesus blessed it, that little lunch not only fed the whole multitude, it fed the little boy too. Filling someone else's need will in turn come back to us from our Heavenly Father and fill the very need that we have.

> *Give, and it will be given to you. A good measure,*
> *pressed down, shaken together and running over,*
> *will be poured into your lap.*
> *For with the measure you use, it will be*
> *measured to you.*
> Luke 6:38

If we know of someone who is sick we could call to see how they are doing, keeping in mind the fact that depending on the circumstances, they might not be up to a long conversation. Take time to say a prayer for their recovery and ask if they would like a visit or if we could bring them some food, run an errand for them, or get some groceries for them. Maybe they would appreciate it if we would come and do a bit of housework or laundry for them if they are not up to it.

When we hear of someone who is feeling down, just a phone call and saying a prayer with them can make all the difference. Just to knowing that someone cares and is thinking about them can lift their saddened heart.

A true witness of what a real Christian is, is going out of our way to help others. Many people outside the church are brought to Christ because someone took the time to show the love of God. Thoughtful deeds open the door to tell people of God's love. It often softens a persons heart, and makes them more receptive to the Gospel.

When a woman in our church had a baby, the ladies got together and made and delivered a dinner for her and her family, every night for a week. When the people in our community heard of this act of kindness that was shown to this new mom, it made a big impression on everyone.

> *By this everyone will know that you are my disciples,*
> *if you love one another.*
> John 13:35

The Bible speaks a lot about helping others, clothing the needy and feeding the hungry. Today there are many government programs to help those in need. We as Christians need to be wise where we do our helping. Helping the needy and helping the lazy are two very different things. We are told in 2 Thessalonians 3:10, *The one who is unwilling to work shall not eat.* We know that there are many people who are truly unable to work, and these people should be helped. But if a person is healthy and not working or not even looking for work, helping them would only enable them to keep on being lazy, which in the long run will hurt them by making them start expecting someone to take care of them with no effort put forth on their part. It will also take away what resources we have to help those who truly do need help.

There is one more very important thing to look at here and that is, we Christians can become so busy helping others that our own families end up being neglected and feeling like they aren't as important as these other people. We must keep this in mind and diligently guard against it. This precious family that God has given us, must always come first to us.

Gift Basket

> *Trust in the Lord, and do good.*
> Psalm 37:3

A few years ago, after I had had some surgery and was recuperating, one of the ladies in our church brought me a beautiful gift basket that the ladies of the church had put together for me. It was so pretty, and it made a lasting impression on me. This deed of kindness touched my heart and cheered me up.

So, I thought we might like to take a look at how easy it is to make a gift basket. Here is another way to show Christian love for those who are sick or in need of encouragement. Putting it together is really an easy thing to do, and there are countless ways to do it. This may be a ministry that you or the ladies in your church would like to fulfill.

Let's say for instance that we are making one for a woman who likes to cook. We could get a cookbook or cooking magazine, and then take the colors from its cover to choose our color for the gift basket. Using a basket or a mixing bowl or even a pretty casserole dish for our container would work quite well, and then we could line it with a matching kitchen towel. Next we might add some specialty vanilla or some spices, maybe some pretty measuring cups or spoons and a nice whisk or a silicone spatula. Lastly add a scented candle, and a few silk flowers or some greenery to add color and brighten up the basket. See how easy this is?

An idea for a woman who likes to read could be created around a book by her favorite author or devotional book. If the cover has something red and white in it, use those colors in the rest of the basket. You might add some tea with a matching teacup or some raspberry jam or small red candies or even fruit if they are not diet restricted. Then use some red and white silk flowers or a candle to brighten up the basket.

A gift basket for a new mom could be made to fit the baby, the mother, or even a bit of both. You could include an outfit, a blanket or a lullaby CD for the baby. For the mother, a devotional book written especially for mothers, some bubble bath, or some sweet-smelling lotion would no doubt be very welcome. You don't have to put all these things in the gift basket these are just a few suggestions.

A gift basket for a man could include a men's devotional book, or if he likes hunting or fishing, a magazine on the subject would be welcomed. If he's a sports fan, something geared to the team he likes would show thoughtfulness to him. How about some coffee and a coffee mug that is in the theme of the sport he likes? Maybe a little greenery would brighten it up.

It doesn't have to be big, just thoughtful. Try to personalize it to fit the person you're giving it to. This is where it really helps to pay attention when people are talking because we all, without knowing it, give away our likes and dislikes.

Dress

She is clothed in fine linen and purple.
Proverbs 31:22

After all, you are the queen of your home.

Having stylish, well-made, well-fitting clothes to wear makes you feel self-assured, and even more energetic. We will feel better about ourselves if we take the time and effort to dress nice and neat no matter what we have planned for the day. Even if our clothes aren't new they should always be clean and neat, no buttons missing, and no hems hanging half-sewn.

I once read that if you are feeling low for any reason, or if you are under some pressure, it's especially important to take the time to dress well and fix your hair and makeup the best you can. Even though you can't change these other things that are happening, knowing that you look good will buoy you up and give you an air of confidence that others around you will see and feel. This will undoubtedly help you handle the situation in the very best way.

> "No matter how you feel,
> get up, dress up, show up,
> and never give up."
> Regina Brett

Get a full-length mirror, so that you can check to see how you look in front and back. If you don't like what you see there, change your clothes until you find something that looks good on you. Get a chair and sit down in front of the mirror, checking how you look in different positions. Then practice sitting in a way that looks modest and attractive. No slouching around; practice good posture.

When you're shopping for clothes, remember that you can't always go by the size that is on a garment. Different manufacturers size their clothes differently. Purchase clothes by how they fit not by the size listed on the tag. No one but you sees the size that your clothes are, but they do see how they fit. Look at clothing that is one size up or one size down from your normal size. There will be many times that these fit and look much better than your normal size.

Many years ago, Edith Head, who was the number one dress designer for the stars, gave this advice about how our clothes should fit us, and these words are still true today. She said, "Clothes should be tight enough to show you are a woman, but loose enough to show you're a lady." This is an excellent standard to hold unto as our own, and our daughter's. Clothes that just skim the body, that don't cling to the body, look better than either clothes that are too tight or clothes that are too loose. If you are overweight and your clothes are overly tight, that fact will be all too obvious for all to see. If you are very thin and your clothes are too tight this also will look bad, making you look like you are ill. As we age, this is even more important.

I was in the restaurant one day and I noticed a woman who was very overweight. But this woman was dressed and groomed so impeccably that instead of thinking how overweight she was, I just thought about how beautifully she was dressed and how she carried herself with such grace. Everything she wore complemented her and took the attention away from her weight, leaving only the thought of how lovely she was.

Learn to dress modestly and still look pretty and stylish. If the skirt or dress is too short, wear some leggings or skinny jeans under it. If the blouse is cut too low, wear a camisole under it that comes up a bit higher.

It honors our husband to dress modestly around others; after all, our body is, *for his eyes only*. How often do we hear of men who talk about other men's wives in an inappropriate way because of the way she dresses. If we dress immodestly around others, they'll talk about us in the same way. Not only that, as Christian women we set an example for younger women, so we must be watchful in the way we dress. Immodest dress sends the wrong message. This displeases the Lord and could cause some men to look at us in a lustful way. We don't want to do anything that would make our Christian brothers or anyone else stumble into sinful thoughts.

Don't just dress to impress others, dress nice for your family. I'm not saying you should wear a ball gown while you are making dinner, but dress nice for your family, and appropriately for what you are doing at the time. After all, our families are the most important people in the world to us. Who better to dress nice for?

Dressing well when we go out, not only makes us feel more confident but it is also a good reflection on our husband. It shows that he has chosen well when he chose us to be his wife. Even if we can't dress in the latest fashion, we can still be neat, clean and wear a sweet smile.

Your Closet

A well-stocked closet is very important. This doesn't mean a huge amount of clothes, it means clothes we actually wear and wear often. This should contain mostly clothes that are timeless in style. Spend most of the money you have for clothes such as: a little black dress, a fitted white blouse, a pencil skirt, a pair of black trousers, a pair of blue jeans that fit just right, a trench coat and a casual jacket, a pair of black pumps, a pair of black flats, and some stylish white tennis shoes. These are the backbone of your closet, and they will last for years to come. Now that we have the basics, let's fill out our closet.

Have you ever gone to your closet and although you see a lot of clothes, you feel like you have nothing to wear? How much better it is to have a few well-made, well-fitting clothes, than to have a closet full of ill-fitting, outdated pieces. I'm going to show you how, with a little imagination and some careful planning, you can take a small amount of clothes and make a lot of different outfits with them making it look like you have a lot of clothes. Then, by adding some matching accessories, you can put together even more outfits.

A good example is the little black dress. It can look nice all by itself, but if you add a pearl necklace, a pretty white shawl, an evening bag, and dressy pumps, you have a very elegant looking outfit. Or pair the dress with a dressy little jacket, matching jewelry, and a handbag, and you have another very nice outfit. You can also pair it with a blue jean jacket, low boots, and a bandana scarf around your neck or your hair and you have put together a casual outfit. All four outfits out of the "little black dress." See how easy it is?

There is one very important thing to consider when building your wardrobe, and that is to make sure the colors you choose goes well with your skin tone. There are two groups of skin tones: one is the warm skin tone and the other is the cool skin tone. The warm skin tone looks best in warm earthy colors that have an underlying yellow tone. Their best colors would be cream, orange, yellow, olive green, turquoise blue, and a yellowy brown. The best metal color would be gold. The cool skin tone looks best in cool colors that have underlying tones of blue, their best colors would be shades of pink, rose red, forest green, royal or denim blue and a grayish brown. Their best metal color would be silver. I've noticed with myself that if I choose colors that lean toward a subtle blue, that my complexion looks rosy and healthy, but if I choose colors that have and underlying coloring of yellow my complexion looks pasty and gray. With this in mind, it's best to keep away from the wrong colors for your complexion, especially the colors you put close to your face.

Remember that day, not long ago, when the outfit you wore felt so right and the pieces seemed to look and feel great together? Remember how you felt more confident, and it even lifted your spirit? There is a way to get the same look and feeling every day with little effort, and it's called creating a wardrobe capsule.

The Wardrobe Capsule

A wardrobe capsule is a way of taking a few pieces of clothing and putting them together in different ways to create many outfits. Let's take a look at how to do this. It's really easier than you might think.

Let's take five items in three colors that look good together and see how to do this. We'll take four solids and one jacket that matches all three colors. Then let's see how many outfits we can make out of them. We can choose any three colors just so they all go good together. In this example, we're going use the colors of black, camel and cream.

We'll start with one pair of cream slacks, one camel-colored skirt, one black top, one cream top and one jacket which matches all three colors. Every piece here will go well with every other piece.

1. The cream slacks with the black top
2. The cream slacks with the black top and the jacket
3. The cream slacks with the cream top
4. The cream slacks with the cream top and the jacket
5. The camel skirt with the black top
6. The camel skirt with the black top and the jacket
7. The camel skirt with the cream top
8. The camel skirt with the cream top and the jacket

Here we have eight different outfits with only five different pieces of clothing. See how easy this is? Now if we just add three more pieces, a pair of camel slacks, a cream skirt, and a camel top, we can make eight more outfits.

9. The camel slacks with the black top
10. The camel slacks with the black top and the jacket
11. The camel slacks with the camel top
12. The camel slacks with the camel top and the jacket
13. The cream skirt with the black top
14. The cream skirt with the black top and the jacket
15. The cream skirt with the cream top
16. The cream skirt with the cream top and the jacket

Now we have sixteen different outfits with only eight pieces of clothing. If we add a pair of black slacks and a black skirt, we will get an additional twelve outfits making twenty-eight outfits with only ten separate pieces. We'll have three pairs of slacks, three skirts, three tops and one jacket.

17. The black slacks with the black top
18. The black slacks with the black top and the jacket
19. The black slacks with the camel top
20. The black slacks with the camel top and the jacket
21. The black slacks with the cream top
22. The black slacks with the cream top and the jacket
23. The black skirt with the black top
24. The black skirt with the black top and the jacket
25. The black skirt with the camel top
26. The black skirt with the camel top and the jacket
27. The black skirt with the cream top
28. The black skirt with the cream top and the jacket

See, this isn't that hard at all. It's just a matter of taking three colors that complement our complexion and each other, then building a wardrobe capsule with them. If we do this, it will take us no time to put an outfit together because no matter what we pick out, it will match everything else we have in our wardrobe capsule. Then, we can choose different styles of clothing in each of these three colors. Blouses can be short sleeved, long sleeved, button up, V-neck, or pullover. Skirts can be a pencil, an A-line, or a flared skirt, you get the idea. No matter how many pieces we have, if we keep them all in our color, whatever we put together will automatically match and look great together.

Let's face it, ladies, we all like clothes, and we want more than just a few pieces and more than just three colors. This is just an example of what you can do with a good imagination and a little creativity. You can make as many separate capsules as you like.

Ok, now it is time to shop your closet. Following the pattern you just read about, you may be surprised to find that everything you need to create your own capsule is right there in your closet, to create your own capsule. Then you can add more pieces as you go, making sure that you are staying in your color.

First you must decide on the three colors you want to use. Don't be alarmed if you find that the clothes in your closet are not in the best color for your complexion. This happened to me. Most of my adult life I wore colors of orange and olive, which I loved, but what I didn't realize at the time was that these colors didn't love me. I wondered why people would often tell me that I looked a bit piqued or would ask me if I didn't feel good when I felt fine. Then, one day I came across a book called *Color me beautiful* by Carole Jackson, and I learned the way to find the right colors for our complexion was to put a piece of material or clothing close to our face, first one that is silver and then one that is gold. When you look in a mirror, you will easily see which one makes your complexion look the best." I didn't have either of these, so I went to a clothing store and took a blouse of each color off the rack, then found a mirror to see which color looked the best for me. To my surprise, it turned out to be silver.

Even if you don't have the best colors for your complexion right now, you can still start putting outfits together with what you do have. This will teach you how to create a wardrobe capsule. Then you can start working toward creating the correct color capsule for yourself.

The first thing to do is to decide on the three colors you want to use, then choose the best five pieces of clothing that you have in those colors: one pair of slacks, one skirt, two tops, and one jacket that matches all three colors.

Next, take out those five pieces, and start putting your wardrobe capsule together. Then, add a few more pieces in your color to fill out your capsule. You can make it as small or as large as you like. When you finish putting your outfits together in your three main colors, you can also add some pieces with graduating colors.

You can create a casual capsule and a dressy capsule. If you do, you will be ready at a moment's notice to go anywhere you want to go, Then when you take a look at the day ahead and see what you're going to do or where you're going to go, you'll know exactly which capsule to choose from.

Don't forget your shoes. Shoes can either pull an outfit together or they can ruin the look that you're going for. Your shoes should be in the same color and style that your clothes are in.

Now, go and see what you can come up with and how many beautiful outfits you can put together. Then you'll be able to easily choose an outfit for the day ahead.

Clothes for Each Member of Your Family

*When it snows, she has no fear for her household;
for all of them are clothed in scarlet.*
Proverbs 31:21

The last thing we're going to look at is another very important thing to do, and that is to make sure you and each member of your family have the right kind of clothes, and the right amount of clothes that they need for everything that they do.

A good way to do this is to make a chart for each member of your family with the days of the week listed across the top of the page and the hours in the day, from the time you get up in the morning until you go to bed at night listed down the left side of the paper. Add lines from side to side separating the hours in the day, and lines from top to bottom separating the days of the week. Now in each box put a letter signifying what kind of clothing you need for that particular block of time. You could use "W" for work, "H" for home, "C" for church, "S" for school, you get the picture.

This will clearly show you where each member of your family needs the most clothes and where they need the least. Now that you've done that, go through your closet and each member of your family's closets, and see if more clothing is needed for any of these categories, or if each one is well supplied in every area. Always remember that dressing well gives everyone, not just adults, a feeling of confidence. When I did this, I found that I had the most clothes for what I did the least, and the least amount of clothes for what I did the most.

Plan ahead and shop for the next season when things are on sale. If your clothes budget is small, check the thrift shops in your area. You will often find new or like-new clothes there at a fraction of the department stores prices.

The thing is, we are always buying something, so let's use the money we have to buy something that we will be happy with for a long time. Settle for less but better.

Chapter 2

The Man of the House

F. Burton once said on the subject of marriage, "If you want something to last forever, You treat it differently. You shield and protect it. You never abuse it. You don't expose it to the elements. You don't make it common or ordinary. If it ever becomes tarnished, you lovingly polish it until it gleams like new. It becomes special because you have made it so, and it grows more beautiful as time goes by."

> *The Lord God said,*
> *It is not good for a man to be alone.*
> *I will make a helper suitable for him.*
> Genesis 2:18

A great marriage isn't something you find,
It's something you create.

In this chapter we'll look at some of the things we can do for our husband to help him realize what a treasure he is to us and to make our marriages not just survive, but thrive. Since he is our closest friend, our most trusted confidante, and the love of our life, we want to do everything we can to show him how much we love and respect him.

The first thing that holds a great amount of importance to men is *respect*. Men need respect far more than we ladies realize. We will see the importance of guarding his name when we talk to others. Then we will be taking a look at the difference in how our husband is treated before the children arrive and how he is treated after. We will also look at how he is greeted when he comes home from work and dressing him for success in whatever job he has. We will look at the problems that arise and how to deal with them in a way that will be fair to both of us. Lastly, we will see how men deal with the *hints* that we ladies like to drop for them. This is a bit like the game we played as children, "A tiskit a taskit, a green and yellow basket." We skip along dropping hints for them, expecting them to pick them up and automatically know what we want them to do with them.

Our husband is, and always will be, the most important adult in our life. I've heard it said that the best gift that parents can give their children is to love, truly love, each other. When children see dad and mom loving each other and consistently showing respect for each other, they will have a great sense of security, which is vitally important for them, especially in this age where divorce seems to be lurking in the shadows of so many homes. It will also show them what true love is and how it acts. It will show them what to look for in the mate that they will one day make a lifetime commitment with, one that has a true heart for God and family.

Above all, love each other deeply.
1Peter 4:8

With that in mind, let's take a look at a few verses in the thirteenth chapter of First Corinthians. Here we will see what real love is and how it acts.

Love is patient, Love is kind.
It does not envy, it does not boast, it is not proud.
It is not rude, it is not self-seeking,
it is not easily angered, it keeps no record of wrongs.
Love does not delight in evil but rejoices with the truth.
It always protects, always trusts, always hopes, always perseveres.
Love never fails.
And now these three remain: faith, hope, love.
But the greatest of these is love.
1 Corinthians 13: 4-8, 13

Respect Is the Most Important Thing to Him.

The wife must respect her husband.
Ephesians 5:33

I don't think this is just a suggestion, do you?

A group of men were asked, "What is the most important thing that their wife could do for them." Their immediate and overwhelming response was; to respect them. It is extremely important for our husbands to know that they are admired as a hero to their family. Since God has appointed them to be the head of the home and leader of the family, they are to be respected as such. God appointed us to not only respect our husband but also to instill that respect for their father in our children. We should never say disrespectful things to him, or about him to our children, this will make them lose respect for him. Also, our children should never be allowed to say disrespectful things to their father or about him. Neither should they be allowed to act in a disrespectful way toward him. If they do any of these things, we must immediately correct them.

Putting your husband first does not diminish the love you feel for your children. It enhances it because your children were born out of that love, and it actually makes that love more evident. If you push your husband down on your list of priorities, your children will believe their father isn't all that important. On the other hand, if they see you honoring their father with the number one spot, they will feel the love and security of a stable home that they will get no other way.

When you put your children, parents, best friends, talents, or career before your husband, you send a clear message to him that he is not as important to you as these other people or these other things are to you. Imagine having that message sent to you day after day for many years. What would that do to your self-esteem?

Recognize and Relate

A wise woman portrays her husband as the hero that he is to her children. If we look for, recognize, and relate to our children the things that their father does that makes him a hero to his family, our children will grow up with a deep respect for him, looking up to him their whole life long. Our daughters will look for the same qualities in the husband that they will one day choose, and our sons will want to pattern their lives after him. Once we start making a point of looking for all the times our husband puts his precious family before himself and goes the extra mile in all he does for them, we will no doubt be amazed at how often he does this.

> "The greatest favor we can give our children is to give a visible example of love and esteem to our spouse. As they grow up, they may then look forward to maturity so they too can find such love."
> Eucharista Ward

Teach your children to love and respect their father. Tell them how smart he is and how much he loves them. Tell them the ways he shows them love without even saying a word. Lead by example, show him that you respect him and value his advice, go to him for advice, and then make sure you take it.

Knowing that he is so much stronger than we are, we should always ask him to help us with the heavy stuff. Commenting on how strong he is, and how thankful we are to have him help us tells him that he is a hero in our eyes. Make him feel special by admiring his abilities. Tell him, "You can do anything." Men love compliments as much as we do. Let him know just how very much he is loved, needed and appreciated. You will not be sorry.

> "A wise woman knows the importance of
> speaking life into her man.
> If you love him: believe in him, encourage him
> and be his peace."
> Denzel Washington

Be his cheerleader, encourage his abilities, and show him that you have faith in everything he does. If he's having doubts about a hard task that he's trying to do, encourage him by reminding him of some of the hard things he has accomplished in the past, and tell him that this too will be another accomplishment to add to that list. Always be in his corner and celebrate his accomplishments, big and small. Small accomplishments should never go unnoticed, and big accomplishments should get even more recognition. Get your children in on the fun of celebrating; they love to have a party. Tell others about it in his presence. Doing this in his presence will mean even more to him. Oh, he may act embarrassed, but believe me, he'll be loving it. As 1Corinthians 8:1 reminds us, *love builds up*. Be his cheerleader!

His Work

President Ronald Reagan once gave wives this insight into a man's thinking. He said, "There is no greater happiness for a man than approaching a door at the end of a day knowing someone on the other side of that door is waiting for the sound of his footsteps."

When a husband comes home from work to find a nicely dressed, sweetly perfumed, and most of all smiling wife to greet him, his stress of the day will lighten. When he sees his happy children anxiously awaiting his arrival and smells the appetizing aroma of dinner cooking on the stove, you will see a light automatically come into his eyes. Seeing how his family looks forward to his homecoming and how important he is to them, will make his day's work not seem so hard. In fact, all that he does to provide for his precious family, will seem well worthwhile to him.

So ladies, before he comes home put on something pretty, run a brush through your hair, and add a spritz of perfume and a little makeup. If he's greeted at the door with a family that shows how happy they are to see him; he will feel like a king.

Teach your children to greet their father with excitement; "Dad's home!" Create that excitement by telling them to wash their faces and put their toys away. Tell them how he has worked hard all day to provide a nice home for them to live in, good food for them to eat, and nice clothes for them to wear. I've known men to say that when they come home from work, there is no one but the dog happy to see him, even when his family is right there. How very sad.

When your husband first arrives home, tired from a day's work, unless it's an urgent need, don't hit him with every problem you've had all day. It's very important that no matter how you feel or how your day has gone that you push your own feelings aside for a little while, and greet your husband with a sweet smile, a smile that says you're happy that he's home. If there are problems with the children or anything else that you have to discuss with him, wait for a little while, maybe even until after dinner, so your husband can have a little time to relax and unwind, then calmly tell him about the problem. He will not only be more receptive, he will also be able to make a better decision after he has rested.

Tell him you appreciate all he does to provide for your family. Tell him how blessed you are because of his wise leadership and how safe you feel with him protecting your family from any harm. Tell him how you miss him when he's gone, and that all day long you look forward to the time when he comes home, and your family can all be together again.

> "He takes care of the country,
> I take care of him."
> Nancy Reagan

Pack him an appetizing lunch to take to work. Plan ahead and make a little extra of your evening meal so you can make him an especially good lunch. Put it in some nice containers that will go in his lunch box to be warmed up. Don't use plastic for things that go into the microwave though, because the oils from the plastic can melt and get into his food. Keep a variety of things that he likes on hand to put in his lunch. If he works where there is no microwave, you can still make him a tasty lunch, like a man-size sub sandwich, some of the chips that he especially likes, and a couple of his favorite pickles or peppers. Get it together as much as possible the night before, and then you'll only have a few last-minute things to do to get it ready in the morning when he needs it. Stick a little love note in it just to remind him that you are thinking of him. Get a good-looking lunch bag to keep his lunch fresh, and one that looks manly to carry. Ged rid of old, worn-out lunch bags or containers. Some of the small coolers will naturally get dirty, but a little scrubbing with some cleanser will have them looking good with very little effort. Keep him looking good right down to the lunch container he carries. Taking care of your husband in this way is another way to show him how much you love and appreciate him.

Always remember that harsh stinging words in the morning will rob your husband of efficiency all day long, while soft, loving words will spur him on to a good day, and make his heart sing. Proverbs 12:25 reminds us that, *Anxiety weighs down the heart, but a kind word cheers it up.*

Dress Him for Success

Dress your husband well. Keep his clothes clean and pressed when needed. When a piece of clothing looks old or worn, unless he really likes it or it has a special meaning for him, replace it with something new.

At a church I attended many years ago, we had a visiting elderly minister who gave the wives of the congregation this advice. He said, "If your husband is in ministry, keep his clothes clean, pressed, and up to date." Then he added that his wife did this for him and it made him feel more confident when he stood before the people to minister. It also showed the congregation the great respect he had for the office the Lord had appointed him to.

Exodus 28 tells us how God wanted the Jewish priests to be dressed because of their high calling, their priestly duties, and their place among the people, all of which were not to be taken lightly. God wanted His priests to be dressed in a way that would bring dignity and honor to them and to the office that they held. They were not to wear clothes that were worn for every day. They had very special clothes to wear when they were performing the duties of the priest of God. They were called sacred garments and every piece of clothing had to look just right.

At the time that God appointed Aaron, the brother of Moses, to be the High Priest of His people, He had a very special way He wanted Aaron to be dressed: *Make sacred garments for your brother Aaron,* [and the reason for it] *to give him dignity and honor* (Exodus 28:2).

When Aaron stood before the people, dressed in his sacred garments, to perform his priestly duties, a silent message was sent to the people that they were to show respect to Aaron as the priest of God. Even in our casual world, this still applies today. God never changes, His messengers still have a high calling, and He still wants them to be given dignity and honor as they perform their sacred tasks. We need to see that they are dressed accordingly. We may not be able to afford expensive clothes, but the Lord does expect us to do the best we can.

This is also good advice if he is in business. The way he is dressed will send the message that he is to be respected, and that he is confident and capable of doing the job at hand. When people see him they judge him by what they see.

If he works in a factory or any other blue-collar job, he will look and feel better about himself if he is dressed well. Blue jeans and a t-shirt may be the appropriate work attire for his job, but keep them looking good, clean, and in good condition. Tell him how good he looks, especially when he's dressed up. Let him know that you notice when he takes special care to look good.

Before the Children

*I went past the field of a sluggard, past the vineyard
of someone who has no sense;
thorns had come up everywhere, the ground was
covered with weeds, and the stone wall*

*was in ruins. I applied my heart to what I observed
and learned a lesson from what I saw:
A little sleep, a little slumber, a little folding of the
hands to rest—and poverty will come
on you like a thief and scarcity like an armed man.*
Proverbs 24:30-32

"A man marries a woman,
hoping she will never change."
Albert Einstein

Before the children come along, we place all our affection on our husband, which of course is what they love. But oftentimes, soon after the first baby arrives our husband falls into second place. After all, he's an adult and he can take care of himself. It's only natural that this helpless little one gets most of our attention, and it does take a lot of time to care for them properly. But all too soon our husband gets less and less attention. He gets pushed aside and this new little one moves to the place he once held, sometimes causing resentment. Of course, our husbands do love their children, and they do understand that childcare is very time consuming, but they want to be shown love too. After all, the reason we have this sweet little one is the result of the love we have for our husband. We may not have as much time as we did before the children came along, but it is crucial to a good marriage to make time to come together as husband and wife.

Often we don't understand that with men, sex is not just a want but a consuming need. It's much more than just the need for physical gratification, it makes a man feel whole down to the very core of his being, and it solidifies the bond and closeness between a husband and his wife. I know what you're thinking, "With all that I have to do around this house to keep things going, I don't have any time or energy left for that, and he should understand." And he probably does, but that consuming longing for you is still there. We really should be thrilled that they actually need us so much. Let's face it, if our child was hungry or crying, even in the middle of the night, we would be right there to take care of them. The same should be true for our dear husbands. They need us, and when their love cup is full they will be glad to help with the children, laundry, or anything else that we need.

Think back to the time when you were first married, when there were just the two of you, and you loved making love to him and doing things for him. Yes, you have a lot more to do now with having a family, but always keep in your heart of hearts that at one time you were his, just his, and he absolutely loved that. So, even though you can't do it as much now, still give him that again and as often as you can. You will be amazed at the change in his attitude toward many things.

Men are visual, and you can direct his vision to you, and you alone. It is up to you to find out what catches his eye and then be his "eye candy". When you are alone, dress in a way that attracts him, and he will love you for it. In fact, that's just what our men need from us. We may not have a perfect body, but let's try to keep it looking as good as we can for him. Men have a driving need for sex, it's just how God designed them. We may need sweet words and cuddling, but they need sex. The more we give them what they need, the more they will, in turn, give us what we need.

They need sex to feel loved and completed. It really makes a man's self-esteem soar when he knows that you not only think he is desirable, but that you also enthusiastically demonstrate it to him. This will make your husband feel like he is blessed beyond measure with you as his wife.

It's really a wonderful thing for both of you. You don't want him to be tempted to look longingly at other women, and when he gets what he needs from you, no other woman will ever be able to draw his attention away from you.

These words of wisdom come to us from Proverbs 27:7 instructing us that, *One who is full loathes honey from the comb*, [she may look good but he's not interested, because his love cup is full], *but to the hungry, even what is bitter tastes sweet*, [even a distasteful woman looks good to him because his love cup is empty]. Let's keep our husbands filled with our love, and then they won't be tempted to get it elsewhere. Keep pouring love into his love cup to keep it full, full, or overflowing!

A love cup can only stay full if we continually keep pouring love into it. Once we stop, it will dry up. Our husband has to be kept number one in our lives. If we tell him how much we love him but don't show him, our words become empty words to him.

So, ladies, flirt with your husband. When you're in a room full of people, catch his eye and give him that look. You know, the one that sends a sweet kiss across the room.

Fake Romance

Spending too much time reading romance novels and watching romantic movies can give a woman an unreal expectation of what life and real love is really like. In these fake romances, the men treat their ladies so romantically that nothing is too good for them. They follow them to the ends of the earth with only one thought in mind, and that is to win the woman's heart. We have to realize that the people in these books and movies are following a script that is designed to draw you in and give you a desire to want more and more of this kind of fake romance. The most important thing that must be remembered about all this is that they are *fiction*, they are just *fantasy*, they are made-up stories, written to entice women. They are only the empty product of someone's overactive imagination.

In real life things are not that way. If we keep thinking they should be, we will be miserable and make our husband miserable too. Yes, we do want to be treated with respect and love, but we have to remember that we get what we give. If we want to be treated well, we must also treat our husband well.

"Happily ever after" is not a fairy tale; it's a choice. It doesn't happen without some diligent searching to find out what to do to bring this about, and then both of you consistently doing it.

We've all seen women who fall for a man who has a way with sweet words but no character, and then they end up supporting him and being mistreated by him.

They find out too late that the sweet words were only a con to get a woman they can control and do their bidding.

We all long for sweet words and romantic treatment, but if we have a good, hard-working husband who truly loves us and our children, we already have an abundance of blessings that many other women truly long for.

Adapt Yourself

A wise thing to do to build closeness in your marriage is to adapt yourself to your husband.

Nancy Reagan knew that President Reagan loved horses, so she took riding lessons so she would be an able rider with him. She adapted herself to what President Reagan liked, and I don't know if there was ever a truer love story than theirs. He adored her and wrote her love letters almost daily.

Learn to like what he likes so you can do a certain amount of things together. This doesn't mean you have to do everything he likes and set aside the things that you like to do. It just means to find some things that are important to him that the two of you can do together.

One of the most important things that makes a family strong is a close relationship between husband and wife. This doesn't happen without some thought and some planning. Take time for just for the two of you. Plan ahead for a date night or afternoon picnic.

Family Budget

Be wise about your finances.

> *The heart of her husband doth safely trust in her,*
> *So that he shall have no need of spoil.*
> *She will do him good and not evil all the days*
> *of her life.*
> Proverbs 31:11 (KJV)

When a wise older woman was visiting our church, she gave this advice to the wives in the congregation. "One of the best things you can do as a wife, is to live within your family's income, without complaining." You show sincere appreciation and respect to your husband by carefully following a budget and making the most of what you have.

Never make remarks about what others have that you don't. Be thankful for what you do have and take good care of it. Spend the money you have wisely and look for ways to save money when you can. Then when you do, don't flaunt it; just know that your husband appreciates all the effort you put forth to work together with him in caring for your family. Our husbands are diligently working at all the hard stuff for us and our children. They would give their life to protect us from anything that would harm us. They do many jobs that are expected, not applauded, just like we do.

Be content with what you have.
Hebrews 13:5

Constantly complaining about not having enough money to fulfill your desires or racking up credit card debt is a poor way of saying thank you to a faithful husband who works hard every day to provide for his family. You may not have enough extra money to buy that designer handbag you've had your eye on, but your husband will appreciate the fact that you honor him by being grateful for what he does provide. If he knows you want that designer handbag, you can count on the fact that he'll be doing everything he can to get it for you.

Problems

> *Moreover if thy brother shall trespass against thee,*
> *go and tell him his fault between thee and*
> *him alone: if he shall hear thee,*
> *thou hast gained thy brother.*
> Matthew 18:15 (KJV)

If your husband is doing something that is hurting you, you will do well to address it privately just between the two of you. Even then there is more than one way to do it. Ephesians 4:15 tells us how we are to voice our opinion if there is a problem, it says to, *Speak the truth in love.*

We're supposed to tell the truth, but the key is to tell the truth, "In love." There was a song that was written by Richard and Robert Sherman and sang by Julie Andrews that gave us some good advice concerning this. One line from this song said, "A spoonful of sugar helps the medicine go down," Here we are instructed to sweetly, and lovingly, tell the truth.

We should not be afraid to voice our opinion or be afraid to speak up when we have a different opinion than our husband has. We have a perfect right to voice our opinion, but it's the way we voice our opinion that makes all the difference. There are three important steps to follow. The first is that we must use the *right words*, the second is to use the *right tone of voice*, and the third is to make sure we have the *right heart attitude*. All three of these steps are very important when we talk to our husband about a problem.

So, with that said, when you need to talk to your husband about a problem, think carefully and prayerfully about the words you are going to use. Then use a few well-chosen words to address the problem. Make it quick and to the point, not a long lecture, speaking with as much kindness as you can to address the problem. There is no place in marriage to be brutally honest. Honest yes, we must always be honest, but brutal, never!

He may not even be aware that what he is saying or doing is hurting you, so tread softly and always be kind. Isn't this how you would want him to approach you if something you were doing was hurting him? Ephesians 4:32 (KJV) admonishes us to, *Be ye kind one to another, tenderhearted, forgiving one another, even as God for Christ's sake hath forgiven you.* This is especially good advice concerning how a husband and wife should treat each other.

There are a lot of things that slide right off a man that we ladies take to heart and are deeply hurt by. Have you ever noticed how men talk to each other? They'll tell the other guy that he's ugly or lazy, and the other guy just laughs it off, sometimes throwing the same thing back. No one gets mad; they just laugh and go on. Men often say things without meaning it, and they automatically know they are just joking around. On the other hand, if a woman would tell another woman she was ugly or lazy, they would most likely be enemies for life, for women say what they mean, and mean what they say.

Don't be quick to get angry in a situation. Check yourself; you may find that you may have done something to bring the situation about. Remember, in Matthew 5:7 that Jesus tells us, *Blessed are the merciful for they will be shown mercy.* In other words, if you give mercy, you'll get mercy. I think Jesus is showing us here the importance of showing mercy to those who hurt us, don't you? We must do the same for others and especially to our precious husband. If you're wrong, admit it and ask him to forgive you. That will make it easier for him to do the same thing if he finds that he is doing something that is hurting you. As we know, when we truly love someone, we never purposely hurt them.

Sometimes we have to decide on purpose not to be angry because when we think things through we know in our heart that what has happened is not that big of a deal. Quite often, our husband has no clue that what he said or did to upset us. If we, on purpose, quit acting mad and giving him the silent treatment (now ladies, you know we do this) it won't be long, and that anger will just fade away. Wouldn't we want to be treated this way if we didn't know why our husband who was angry with us? Don't our precious husbands deserve to be treated the same?

Another thing we could do is to remember how fast we could get over our anger if some of our friends stopped by unexpectedly. We would quickly put our anger aside and put a big smile on our face before greeting them at the door.

Staying calm and speaking in a calm, soft voice will go a long way in bringing peace to your home. When you first feel an argument starting to heat up, a couple of ways to defuse it are to either quickly change the subject or even make an excuse to leave the room for a few minutes. If necessary, you can come back later and address the situation when you have both calmed down.

Proverbs 18:21 tells us, *The tongue has the power of life and death.* This verse tells us the enormous amount of power that the tongue has, and we can use our words to either heal or hurt those we love. The choice is ours. The life or death of a relationship is usually brought about by the words that are spoken. Once angry, hurtful words are said, they can be forgiven, but they won't be forgotten. They will still carry their painful sting to the person who they were said to, and many moments of regret to the person who said them.

We all, at one time or another, have had hurtful words said to us, and some of those words have caused very deep wounds. Sometimes we are the ones who, out of anger, say hurtful words to those we love. We can be sure that the devil will bring back the painful sting of those words over and over in our mind and to those we have hurt, because he enjoys hurting us and causing a division between us. When the devil does this, if we decide on purpose to forgive the person who said those words, as many times as the devil shoots those *fiery darts* (Ephesians 6:16 KJV) of hurtful words to our mind, we will find that over time they will hurt us less and less and eventually they will lose their power to hurt us at all. I often wonder if this is what Jesus was talking to Peter about in Matthew18:21-22 (KJV) when they had this conversation about forgiveness.

> *Then came Peter to him, and said, Lord, how oft shall my brother sin against me, and I forgive him? till seven times?" Jesus saith unto him, "I say not unto thee, Until seven times: but, Until seventy times seven.* Matthew 18:21-22 (KJV)

Seventy times seven times is a lot of times to forgive someone over one offense. But even though we say we forgive, often times in our heart those angry feelings keep coming back again and again. So we have to keep forgiving them over and over until, in our heart, those angry feelings are gone.

Never pay back evil for evil and be quick to forgive and forget. We have already read how love acts in 1 Corinthians 13, but I think it would be good to take another look at verse 5. It says, *It* [love] *is not easily angered,* [and especially] *it keeps no record of wrongs.* How often do we bring up past hurts in the heat of an argument? Our husbands very seldom do that. If we stop and remember how many times our dear husband has forgiven us or overlooked something we did or said, we would be much more willing to forgive him for any unkind word or deed.

When we're looking for an answer on how to address a certain problem, there are two scriptures that give us some wise counsel. The first is Nehemiah 2:4-5, *Then I prayed to the God of heaven, and* [then] *I answered the king.* The second is, Proverbs 21:1 (KJV): *The king's heart is in the hand of the Lord, as the rivers of water: he turneth it whithersoever he will.*

Here the Bible tells us of Nehemiah, who was a high official for the king of Persia. Even though he held a high position, he still had to have special permission to make a request of the king. Nehemiah had heard that the wall that surrounded Jerusalem had been broken down by the enemies of the Jews, and he wanted permission to go and lead the Jewish people in repairing it.

At that time, the Jews had many enemies who had ravaged their city, broken down their city's wall and burned their gates, leaving them with little defense against them. These enemies didn't want the wall repaired. Nehemiah knew it would be a dangerous mission, but he still wanted to go to Jerusalem and get it done, for the safety of the Jewish people who lived there. He also knew that the king's heart was in the hand of the Lord to answer yes or no, so before he went to the king, he went to the Lord in prayer.

The Lord is telling us here the proper order in approaching any problem that may arise. Before we are to talk to our husband about a problem, we are instructed to talk to the Lord. If we are the queen of our home then our husband is the king. With that in mind, his heart is in the hand of the Lord. If we do our part by talking the problem over with the Lord first, He will impress on our mind what we should do to best deal with the problem.

There may be times when we pray, that we find that the Lord will give us an answer or an idea that is much better than what we had planned. He may give us advice through His Word that is the exact answer to our problem, or He may speak to us through the *still small voice* deep in our heart, which is spoken of in 1Kings 19:12, and we'll know that it was a word from Him. When we pray we must keep our eyes, ears, and hearts open, expecting, watching, and listening for an answer.

When we pray, sometimes God changes our heart and gives us a different perspective on what is happening that will change our feeling completely. Sometimes He may change our husband's heart. Then there are times when He will take care of the problem, working out the situation without us saying a word. We just have to do what God impresses on our heart in talking to Him first, and by obeying the directions He gives us. Then trusting Him to do whatever else needs to be done that will be fair to both of us. We always get the best results if we follow this pattern with any situation we have to deal with.

We know that men can't read our mind and quite often they have no idea what has upset us. The phrase,

"If you don't know, I'm sure not going to tell you," Is used all too often in marriage. Most of the time, they honestly don't know. Maybe we are looking at it in a different way than he is. We can speak without yelling or being harsh or uncaring.

Both husbands and wives are entitled to their opinion, but we must remember one thing: God has appointed our husband as the leader of our family and the head of our home. There are very few husbands who would purposely make a decision that would harm us or their children in any way.

Being Right

Being right is highly overrated. If you find out that you are, unless it is something very important, let it go. What difference does it really make if it was a red or blue car in the story he told? A wise woman knows when her husband remembers the story or situation a little differently from she does, that she doesn't have to override him with the way she remembers it. A loving wife never makes her husband feel foolish on purpose, and especially not in front of others; that hurts twice as bad.

"To keep your marriage brimming with love in
the wedding cup,
Whenever you're wrong, admit it; whenever
you're right, shut up."
Ogden Nash

One more thing to consider is, what if he is right? This has happened to me more than once, and it is quite embarrassing, especially if you're so very sure that you're right like I was. On one occasion it actually turned out to be a bit of a funny story. We were visiting one of our family members who was in the hospital and we were required to wear a face mask to visit them as not to spread germs. I got myself a mask, put it on, and then I got one for my husband. Next, I proceeded to tell him how to put it on. I didn't think he was understanding my instructions and told him he had it on backwards. To that he replied, "I have it on just like yours." Then I realized, to my great embarrassment, that I was the one with it on backwards. Everyone got a good laugh over it, and with a very red face, I laughed too.

Marriage is not a competitive sport.

Love has responsibilities. There is no place in marriage for competition. Love applauds the other's abilities. In fact, competition is one of the major things that can wreck a loving relationship. One-upping your husband is a very cruel thing to do. So, what if there is something you can do better than he can. Most likely he already knows it, so encourage his abilities, let him be the one to shine, especially in public. He will love you for it.

Nagging is another thing that is totally uncalled for in marriage. It is especially hurtful and embarrassing when done in front of others. This wonderful man who we chose to be our life's mate, who is the father of our children and the one we always run to for help, is not our child or our employee. To treat him like he is, like he can't do anything right, will crush his spirit and eventually stop him from doing anything at all to help us. Can we blame him? Would we want to be scolded every time we decided to do something the way *"we"* thought it should be done?

There was a time when I was in the home of a young couple and the wife was very angry because her husband had loaded the dishwasher wrong; maybe not wrong, but not the way she wanted it to be done. She was slamming the dishes around and growling away as she reloaded it, and I thought to myself, "What difference did it make as long as it was loaded and the dishes came out clean?" The poor guy probably felt like not loading it at all because it looked like no matter how he did it, it was wrong anyway. There is always more than one way to do things, and sometimes we find out, to our great surprise, that he may have a better way of doing things than we do if we'll just give him a chance. Even if it isn't better, just different, is it really worth belittling the one we love over it?

A woman's attitude toward her husband and children sets the mood for the home. Having the attitude of, " If mama ain't happy, ain't nobody happy" or, "happy wife, happy life" is definitely not the right attitude to bring about a happy, peaceful home. How very sad that a woman would be so self-centered that she would make her husband or family miserable if she didn't get her own way.

Since women's lib started, many women have become harsh and hard, demanding their own way, caring little about its effects on their children or their husband. Husbands who once were respected as the protectors and heroes of their wives and children are now often counted as nothing more than a paycheck, not really needed by the family. How often do we hear women say, "It's my way or the highway"? This self-centered attitude will shipwreck a marriage and a family. I'm sure this grieves God's heart, and it has taken a drastic toll on the family unit.

Guard His Name

> *A good name is more desirable than great riches.*
> Proverbs 22:1

Honor your husband in the way you speak about him to your family and friends. Never let disagreements at home be told to others. These disagreements will pass, and then you will wish that you hadn't mentioned them to anyone. If you do tell others about them, it will make them think less of him. They in turn will probably start talking about him behind his back. This is definitely not something you want to happen. We don't want our husband, whom we love so much, to be looked down upon by others.

> "There are few things more frightening to a
> man than giving his heart.

And there are few things more comforting to a man than to know the woman he gave his heart to will protect it with her life."
Fawn Weaver

Our husband needs to know that he can talk to us about anything without worrying that it will go any further or that he will get a condemning lecture from us. We all need understanding, and sometimes we just need our most trusted friend to listen as we unburden our heart.

The heart of her husband doth safely trust in her.
Proverbs 31:11 (KJV)

If our husband has any shortcomings we should always cover him with our love by not telling others about them. This is not to say that if he is abusive we excuse it or hide it; we are talking here of shortcomings that we all have of one kind or another. Let's face it ladies, we have our shortcomings and make mistakes that we would be embarrassed if others knew about. If our precious husband isn't perfect, we don't flaunt that imperfection for anyone else to see. We should keep it to ourselves and ask God to help him in this area Hopefully our husband will do the same for us.

It [love] *always protects.*
1 Corinthians 13:7

Mr. Fix-It

Men always want to fix things. God made them that way. If we tell them a problem, they'll tell us how it can be fixed. From their point of view, this is why we tell them about the problem in the first place. If we are constantly badgering them with complaints, they will try for a while to fix what they can, but if we keep it up, and they can find no solution, out of frustration they will give up and shut us out thinking there is no way they can please us. From a woman's point of view, we just want them to listen and sympathize with us. So, unless you want to know what to do to fix a problem, you'll be better off keeping it to yourself.

Hints

> "If you don't ask, the answer is always, no."
> Carla Ingram

If we want something or we want to do something, usually all we have to do is mention it to our husband and if it's in his power to do so, he will get it for us, or do it for us. Our husbands really do want to please us, the problem is they can't read our mind. They honestly do have our best interest at heart. We often think that if we just give them a hint of what we want, that they should understand that hint, and do it for us. Or that they should just know without us even telling them. In doing this we are only fooling ourselves and bringing a lot of confusion and hard feelings into the relationship. We don't have to make a big deal out of it, usually just mentioning what we want is all we have to do. I've found that if I don't get a definite yes or no, that my husband is thinking about how he can do this for me. So remember, that most likely your husband's answer to your request is yes.

Now ladies, listen up to the voice of experience, this is very important information. *Men do not get hints.* We do, and we think if we do and they don't, then they are ignoring us and not caring about what we want. That is usually not the case, they're just not wired that way. God has given men some gifts that we don't have, so that they can fulfill their role as a man. And God has given us some gifts that men don't have, so that we can fulfill our role as a woman. One gift that God has given women is a sixth sense, what is often called, "A woman's intuition." That's why we can pick up on things so easily. This is a gift that God has given us that men don't have. I believe that God gave us this "woman's intuition" because we are the ones who do most of the nurturing for our children no matter how old they are. Therefore we need to be able to read what is going on with our children, when no words are said.

Our husbands get very frustrated trying to figure out what we would like, and then if they do get us something and we don't like it or say we do but they never see us using it or wearing it, they feel like they've failed. How much better to plan ahead when we have a birthday or some other occasion coming up? Tell him exactly what you would like and describe it in a way he will easily understand, or show him a picture of it, he'll love you for it.

When he does get you something that you're not overly fond of, still wear it or use it once in a while. This will show him that you appreciate his thoughtfulness.

I was talking to a few friends one time about gift giving and I said that my husband and I had decided to tell each other what we want for each occasion that comes up, no hinting around, just plain and simple. Usually I have mine planned way in advance (smile.) The men in the group immediately responded with, "I sure wish my wife would do that!" So ladies, let's quit playing games that don't work, and help our husbands out, because they really do want to please us.

Men, just like us, need to feel that they can please their mate. If not, this can cause a wedge of resentment between husband and wife and start the process of drifting apart. We certainly don't want that to happen. We must vigilantly guard against feelings of bitterness or resentment between us and our precious husbands.

So ladies, admire your man, let him know how important he is to you. You'll see light come into his eyes as he comes to realize that, to you, he is the most important adult in your world.

Then, in turn, you will become the most important adult in his world too.

Chapter 3

The Children of the House

"Children don't come with an instruction book,
they come with a mother."
Unknown Author

"Only God Himself fully appreciates the
influence of a Christian mother in the molding
of character in her children."
Billy Graham

For many years I have observed families and how parents have raised their children. Those who have embedded the Word of God into their children by diligently training them in the Christian faith and values and those who haven't. Herein I have aspired to glean the good things that have proven to bring good results in family life and how children have turned out as a result of their diligence. Even then, when everything was done right, there is that child who for some reason may turn to a prodigal lifestyle and away from their Christian upbringing. That's when we must have faith in the spiritual seeds we've planted in our children's heart, for sooner or later they will surely start to grow and lead them back to God. Should this happen it will be important to show our children that we love them and keep our Christian influence in their life. If they are not around our Christian influence, the enemy will make sure they are around someone who will cast their sinful influence on them. No matter what they do or where they go, to the best of your ability, keep the line of communication open so they can come to you and talk to you about what is going on in their life without being condemned or rejected.

> Proverbs 22:6 reminds us of this promise from God, *Start children off on the way they should go, and even when they are old they will not turn from it.* God told Abraham to *direct his children and his household after him to keep the way of the Lord by doing what is right and just* (Genesis 18: 8-19).

The same mandate that God gave to Abraham, He has given to us: to direct our children and our household, to obey and honor Him.

No one else cares for our children as much as we do. We can't count on someone else to take the time to study the scriptures and to pass on to our children the truths of God's Word or to pray like we would for our children.

We must be the one, not their Sunday school teacher nor the pastor. We must do it ourself.

> *You shall teach them* (God's laws) *diligently to your children, and shall talk of them when you sit in your house, when you walk by the way, when you lie down, and when you rise up.*
> Deuteronomy 6:7 (NKJV)

Those who have the greatest spiritual influence on children are their parents. The home, not the church, *must* be the primary place for Christian education. Spiritual training should be home centered, and church supported.

> Your influence as a mother is powerful.
> Don't waste it; little eyes are watching.

With each child comes a great responsibility, not only to care for, feed, and clothe them but an even greater responsibility to teach each child that has been entrusted into our care by our Heavenly Father, to love and serve Jesus, training them from a very young age that Jesus loves them.

Our children are precious gifts given to us by our Heavenly Father, and He has a special place in His heart for each one of them. He diligently seeks to find just the right parents to give each child to. He could have given them to any parent in the world, but He has given these precious little ones to us. This proves that God trusts us to care for them and train them to follow Him.

The Children of the House

Some people say their child wasn't planned, or they were just an accident. That is far from true. Oh, it may be true that *they* didn't plan on having the child, but the child's Heavenly Father has had their life planned from the beginning of time. Each one has a special purpose and God has a good plan already laid out for their life. We as their parents are part of that plan. We have the awesome responsibility of raising these precious gifts from God to be kind, honest, responsible, and, most of all, godly people.

Jeremiah 1:5 confirms this by saying, *Before **I formed you** in the womb **I knew you**, before you were born **I set you apart**.*

Teaching Children about God

We need to provide our children spiritual food from God's Word. It should be prepared for them in a way they can easily understand it so they will know how to apply it to their life. When our children are small, we prepare food for them that is nourishing yet easy for them to digest to make their little bodies grow healthy and strong. Where a teenager can eat and enjoy a hamburger, a baby has to be fed things that are mashed and strained, like carrots and pears. Likewise, with spiritual food it is necessary to feed each one according to their ability to understand it.

It is our responsibility to teach our precious little ones to love and obey God. If we live like God is important to us, they will grow up believing that He is important to them too. If they see by our actions and deeds that we love and obey God, they will grow up loving and obeying Him also. The opposite is also true.

My parents molded a consistent Christian life to me and my brothers and sisters. They took us to church regularly and had family devotions with us. They modeled the importance of reading the Bible and praying. As I was growing up, I remember coming into the kitchen in the morning and finding my mother sitting at the breakfast table with a cup of coffee and studying her Bible. She treasured God's Word and often talked of finding a "golden nugget," which was a scripture that stood out to her and would encourage her or give her some direction with any problem that she might have and that she felt would give her greater insight in living a life pleasing to God. Now I do the same thing myself, and my grown children say they remember seeing me reading my Bible and praying too. Make a point of letting your children see you reading your Bible and praying. This will leave a lasting impression on them, like it did for me, and they will want to do the same thing themselves.

Have Bible devotions with your children. The book of Proverbs is the book of wisdom and is an excellent book that teaches many lessons on how to please God and how to have a good life. Read it slowly and take time to explain the meaning of each verse in a way they will understand. Then, when they need them, the scriptures you have taught them, will come back to their mind and help them make good decisions. For as David reminds us in Psalm 119:105, *Your word is a lamp for my feet, a light on my path.*

To give our children a good spiritual foundation, it's important to teach them to read and memorize scriptures for themselves when they can. Today we are blessed to have Bibles that are written in a way that is easy to understand for each age group. This means we can get them a Bible that is geared to their ability to read and understand. The youngest children will need one that has mostly pictures, and then as they grow and are able to read and understand more for themselves, they can graduate to Bibles for kids, then junior high Bibles, then finally to Bibles for teens and young adults.

Giving Their Heart to Jesus

When they are young, it's important to use every opportunity you have to teach them about God's love for them, about salvation, and of His forgiveness when they do something wrong.

When they are old enough to understand the concept of salvation, lead them to give their hearts and lives to Jesus. When leading them to Christ, use age-appropriate ways to explain it to them. What a six-year-old will understand and what a teenager will understand are two very different things. When you're reading the Bible to your children, explain to them that sin is breaking God's laws. Use the Ten Commandments as a reference point and tell them that these are God's laws, then ask them if they have broken any of them. Even a small child will understand lying.

An example you could use for this is; if they tell a lie to you and say their homework is done when it isn't. The next day when they go to school their teacher will find out their homework wasn't done, so they will have to stay in for recess to do their homework and they won't be allowed to go out and play with their friends.

Now they have six consequences for one lie:
1. They get scolded by their teacher.
2. They must stay in during recess.
3. They can't go out and play with their friends while the other kids do.
4. They must bring a note home to their parents saying that they didn't do their homework.
5. They will most likely get in trouble with their parents.
6. They still have to do their homework.

Use the word *sin*; people don't want to use that word any more. They are afraid it might make someone feel bad, but we must feel bad about sin, because feeling bad is what leads us to repentance. If we don't feel truly sorry for our sin, how can we truly repent?

A Prayer of repentance for children

> Dear Lord Jesus, I know that I am a sinner, and I ask you to forgive me of my sins. I believe you died on the cross for my sins and rose form the dead. I turn from my sins and I ask you to come into my heart. I want

to follow you as my Lord and Savior all the days of my life. Amen

When they do this, have a celebration. Make a special meal. Do something that they will remember to celebrate the day that they became a Christian. Call Grandpa and Grandma or someone to tell them the good news. Make a certificate to hang on their wall.

Repentance

Even after we give our heart to Jesus, we sometimes do something wrong. It is also very important to teach our children that if they do make a mistake and do something wrong, they can ask God to forgive them, and He will. One of the most important things we must teach our children is that there is *always* a way back to Jesus if they've done something wrong. It's called repentance. No matter what they've done, if they repent, God will forgive them with open arms. There still may be some natural consequences for their wrongdoing they have to deal with, but in God's sight they are already forgiven and made right.

1 John 2:1 says, *My dear children, I write this to you so that you will not sin. But if anybody does sin, we have an advocate with the Father—Jesus Christ, the Righteous One.* An advocate is defined in the dictionary as a lawyer who defends someone in court. Jesus is the one who goes to the Father on our behalf.

Psalm 103:11-13 assures us that when we repent of our sins, Jesus forgives us and wipes the slate clean: *For as high as the heavens are above the earth, so great is his love for those who fear him; as far as the East is from the West, so far has he removed our transgressions from us.* Then He reassures us that He loves us and always will. To repent means to not only be sorry for our sins but to turn from them and do what is right in God's sight.

Teach Us to Pray

Teach your children to pray simple but sincere prayers and to add to them anything they, or someone they know needs prayer for. For example, when they get done saying their prayers, they could add, "Also Lord, would you please heal sissy of her cold," or "Would you help me to remember all I need to remember for the spelling test tomorrow?"

While they are still young, teach them to pray for themselves, because you never know when they will be somewhere by themselves and need to call on God for help. If they have trouble obeying Dad and Mom they could ask Jesus to help them learn to obey. If they are sick they could ask Jesus to help them get better. Teach them that He is always with them and that they can call on Him for help any time, day or night, if they need to, if they are ever afraid of something, a good scripture for them to learn is, Isaiah 41:13, *Do not fear; I will help you.* Put it in a language that is easy for them to remember. For instance, "God is right here to help me, so I won't be afraid." Tell them that God has His guardian angels watching over them and protecting them every day of their life.

Jesus, Their Friend

Teach them that Jesus is their best friend, and that He will always help them with whatever they are doing if they just ask Him. Teach them that He loves them and always will, no matter what. Even if there are times He doesn't like what they do, He will always love them, just like you do.

There are many ways to plant the Word of God in our children's heart.

Spiritual Seeds

While our children are young, we need to plant the Word of God in their hearts and teach them the importance of living for Jesus. If we do this, when they get older and go out into the world and begin to hear negative, sinful things, they will already have a strong spiritual foundation to help them stand strong for Jesus. The spiritual seeds that are planted in the fertile soil of a young heart will never cease to grow.

My word that goes out from my mouth: It will not return to me empty,
but will accomplish what I desire and achieve the purpose for which I sent it.
Isaiah 55:11

If you get a Bible story book that has colorful pictures, it will keep your children's attention, and they will want you to read it over and over to them, implanting the Word of God into their little hearts and minds. Cuddle up together with them in a chair, and read the stories of the Bible together.

After you read the story, talk to them about what the story is telling them, and then ask them, "What have you learned from this story?" Make sure they understand the true meaning of it. Teaching them diligently is very important. Teach them not only the stories of the Bible, but the truths and the principles of God's Word that are found in each story.

When they are learning to read, get them some easy-to-read Bible story books to practice on. This will not only help their reading skills, but it is another way to plant the Word of God in their tender hearts and minds. Decide what you want them to learn and then choose a storybook that teaches that very thing, making sure the storyline in the book lines up with what is written in the Bible.

Also, look for some secular story books that your young children will enjoy, some that teach them good life principles. One that my children loved was, The *Little Engine That Could*. One of the things it teaches is that even though a job may seem too hard to do at first, if we try really hard we are able to accomplish far more than we thought possible.

When my children were little, I read this book to them, but I didn't realize the lasting impression it would have on me so many years later. When I went to work on the line in the factory, I often felt overwhelmed at the immensity of the job I was on, but then a little rhyme from this book would come into my mind. "I think I can, I think I can, I think I can," and pretty soon I would start saying it over and over, and that just seemed to build the confidence I needed to help me keep up on my job just like I was expected to do.

Fun

Kids need to have some time for fun and games, but the time when they are young and teachable goes by very quickly. It's easier to train and nurture a young child than it is to win back a rebellious teenager.

Get a collection of Christ-centered cartoons and movies for them to watch. My grandchildren watched the "Veggie Tales" cartoons, which had important life lessons from the Bible and were also very entertaining for them. There are a lot of good Christian cartoons for young children, and when they watch these they are not only entertained but are taught about God and also learn some valuable life lessons.

Find some fun ways to learn the Bible stories. Do some play acting to make them come to life for your children. But be sure to get what you want them to learn from the story across to them in a way that they will understand and hopefully retain. When the story or play acting is done, ask them what they have learned and how it can be applied to their life. Many times, young children must be told the same thing over and over, so they understand and remember what they have heard.

Songs

Words put to music are easier to remember.

You can also take a scripture that you want your children to learn and put it to a little tune they already know. This will make it easier for them to remember. I still remember a scripture I learned at a very young age that was put to a melody and it has stayed in my heart and mind all these years. It's Ephesians 4:32, *Be kind and compassionate to one another, forgiving each other, just as in Christ God forgave you.* This scripture song tells us that we are not only to be kind to others, but since God has forgiven us, we should also forgive others if they have hurt us in some way. You can see what a great message this song will put in a young heart.

In Exodus 15:1 (KJV) we are told of Pharaoh's army that was pursuing the children of Israel to drive them back into slavery and how God stepped in and drowned them all in the Red Sea. Here is the first verse of the song they sang: *Then sang Moses and the children of Israel this song unto the Lord, and spake, saying, 'I will sing unto to Lord, for he hath triumphed gloriously: the horse and his rider hath he thrown into the sea.'* God instructed the children of Israel to sing this song, so that their dramatic rescue was firmly and permanently set in their minds and passed on to the minds of their children so they, too, would never forget it.

There are many songs children learn in Sunday school, and I'm sorry to say some of them don't make a bit of sense or teach them anything. One song my children were taught was a song with motion:

> There was a wise old king, who had ten thousand men,
> He marched them up a hill one day, and marched them down again.
> And when you're up you're up, and when you're down you're down,
> But when you're only half way up, you're neither up or down.

They did get a bit of exercise going up and down, but how much better it would have been if it was a song that was used to plant God's Word in their little minds?

> *For I know the plans I have for you, declares the Lord, plans to prosper you and not to harm you, plans to give you hope and a future.*
> Jeremiah 29:11

Be very diligent to plant seeds of greatness in your children. Tell them that they have a great life ahead of them. Always encourage them and tell them they can do anything they set their mind to if they don't give up. Tell them repeatedly that God has a great plan for their life. Encourage them to dream big dreams as they plan their future. Always be their encourager and the one who demonstrates faith in them and in their ability.

"It's easier to build up a child
than to repair an adult"
Fredrick Douglas

Words

*The wise woman builds her house,
but with her own hands the foolish one tears
hers down.*
Proverbs 14:1

When I was very young, my father and grandfather built a home for our family. But when the house was finished and no closet was built in the bedroom for her girls, my mother, who was a "git-er-done" kind of a gal, went and bought the material and built it herself. She was amazing. She also built up her whole family with the way she talked to us. She knew the importance of her children having a good self-image. She was indeed a woman who built up her household.

Children automatically believe everything you tell them, so speak good qualities into their lives. Keep your eyes and ears open for every chance you get to tell your children things like "you are thoughtful, you are honest." Making positive remarks when you see them doing something good, will encourage them to repeat the same action. For instance when you see them playing nice with their brother or sister, tell them, "I'm so glad that you two are such good friends." If you do this repeatedly, you'll soon find that they will believe that they are good friends too, and then they are more likely to say that they are and act accordingly.

When we talk to our children, it's easy to add words of praise and encouragement.

Make a list of things you want your children to believe about themselves. They may not have these qualities right now but planting these thoughts in their minds will help bring them into reality.

Here are a few to start with. Every day have them say with you or after you things like, "I am smart, I learn easily, and I remember what I learn, I am kind, I get along well with everyone." You'll be planting seeds of kindness and self-confidence into their hearts and minds, and soon they'll be acting on them and you'll find that they are what you have been saying about them.

The tongue has the power of life and death.
Proverbs 18:21

If we continually say negative things like "can't you two get along?" or "can't you do anything right?" it won't be long until our precious children will believe they really can't get along together, or that they really can't do anything right, and they'll give up trying. Never tell them they are dumb, they will never change, or their life will always be bad. Our words can either build up our children and give them confidence and good self-esteem, or tear them down until they feel like they are worthless. The choice is ours, so we must choose our words carefully. It will make all the difference in our children's life. We must keep a constant watch over the words we say to them.

Inner Voice

It is important to remember what we say to our children will eventually become their inner voice. Think about it, hasn't what was spoken to you as a child become your inner voice? What do you want your children's inner voice to tell them? Speak loving, positive things to them and about them, so their inner voice will build them up, not tear them down. Feed them hope, feed them faith, feed them love.

Use a soft, loving voice as much as possible when talking to your children. Using a loud voice when talking to a child will come across to them as an angry, scolding voice, making them afraid. We definitely don't want our children to live in fear.

Cheerleader

> "Every child needs a champion, an adult who will never give up on them."
> Rita F. Pierson

We are either our children's cheerleader, constantly building them up with positive reinforcing words, or we are the foolish woman who tears down her family's confidence in themselves by constantly making negative, hurtful remarks. Even if we're not saying negative, hurtful words to tear them down, are we building them up with positive encouraging words? You see, the words we choose to say to our children can either build them up emotionally or tear them down.

Our words help set the direction for our children's life.

The good news is if we have been tearing them down with our words, or just not saying words of encouragement to them, we can change our words and we will soon see a change in their attitudes and behavior. It's to our advantage to build our family up and be their cheerleader. This will result in a happy confident family and a happy, peaceful home. If we continually tear them down it will build up anger, resentment, and rebellion in them. Which one would you rather have in your home?

Listen

> "Having a parent who listens, creates a child who believes he or she has a voice that matters in the world."
> Rachel May Stafford

The more you listen to your children, the more you'll learn how they think about things and what is going on in their lives. Sometimes just taking time to play a game together or doing a household task together gets them talking about the things that are on their mind. Quite often we have to talk to them for a while before they start opening up to us. So we need to pay close attention to what they say because children are often afraid to voice their opinion or let us know that they have a different way of looking at things than we do, and they are afraid of being condemned for their opinion if they tell us what it is. We need to be extra diligent in listening to them and helping them make the right decisions that will guide them along the right path.

If we give our children the attention that they need, they are far less likely to look for it in the wrong places.

Talents

God has given us all talents and skills of one kind or another, something that we are naturally drawn to. They come to us as a seed, and it's up to us to cultivate them, and with God's help, make them grow.

Diligently watch to see what areas your children are gifted in. Do they have something they especially like doing and are good at? If so, encourage it. Help them to do good in this area. If they need some training you can't give them, get them into some classes to help develop their skill. Don't let their talents remain as unmined treasures.

Show Love with Your Actions

No matter how we feel,
we are always responsible for how we act.

Make it a practice to smile at your children. This sends a message to them that they are loved, accepted, and that you are glad they are part of your family. When you smile at your children, your face becomes their favorite face to see.

"To the world you may be just another mother,
but to your family, you are their whole world."
Unknown Author

There are times when it's especially important to greet your children with a smile. Times like when you first see them in the morning, or when they first come home from school. They may have had a bad day and your smiling face will lift their spirits. Any time that you have been apart for a while, even if you don't feel like smiling, smile anyway because the face you greet your family with reassures them you are happy to see them and you love them. It will make all the difference in the world to them and set a good atmosphere in your home.

Cherish

Our children will always cherish us if they know, without a doubt, that we truly cherish them. It is essential they know that they and their father are the most important people in the world to us.

Don't push them to grow up; protect their childhood as it will be gone all too fast. There will be many, many years for them to be an adult.

Trust

You and your children may live in the same house, but that alone doesn't produce a close relationship. A close relationship with our children is something that has to be built. It doesn't happen automatically. It takes time and patience to develop, but it pays big dividends. We must be diligent to show them we only want the best for them, demonstrating to them that our advice is valuable.

We must work to build their trust in us so they know they can come to us at any time and tell us their problems without being condemned or rejected for it. If we do this, even though there are rules they have to follow, it won't cause them to be rebellious. We also need to instill in them a respect for us because after all, we are their parents. God has given us the responsibility as parents not only to take care of them and protect them but also to teach them how to make good choices that will lead them to a good and happy life.

Repeat

My mother once told me that if we repeat a phrase or certain words enough, we will find that our family will pick up on them and start saying the same thing. I tried this just to see for myself and it was very true. Whenever something good happened I would say, "Thank You Lord." It seemed like no time before I started hearing my family say, "Thank You Lord" when they had something good happen to them. Start saying things like, "Thank you Lord for the new day you gave me," or when something good happens, they see you, look up and say, "That was You, wasn't it Lord?" This will help them recognize the blessings they are given instead of overlooking them or taking them for granted. It's easy for any of us to overlook the abundance of blessings we've been given every day. My mother gave us children an awe of nature as we grew up without even knowing it just by the way she talked about the beauty of God's creation. I also passed it on to my own children in the same way without realizing what I had done. Put an awe of God's creation in your children's hearts by pointing out and saying things like, "Look at that beautiful sky, the silver lining on the clouds are so beautiful."

Here are a few phrases we can repeat over and over until they are implanted in our children's hearts and minds that will help them know how to conduct themselves and how to act toward others.

We can say things like:

Our family always tells the truth.
Our family always says please and thank you.
Our family always speaks with kindness.
Our family never talks bad about another person.

Then there are family habits that can be reinforced by repeatably saying:

Our family always makes our bed in the morning.
Our family always puts our dirty clothes in the hamper when we take them off.
Our family always puts our dishes in the dishwasher after we are done eating.
Our family always cleans up any mess we make, we never leave it for others to clean up.
Our family makes sure our own jobs are done well, and we don't tell others how to do theirs.

And then there are a couple of little, brush-your-teeth sayings, that we can say with a smile:

Only brush the ones you want to keep,
Only floss the ones you want to keep.

This would even make a good wall plaque to put in the bathroom by the sink.

Conduct

> Your children, will become what you are,
> so be what you want them to be."
> Unknown Author

Kindness

Teach your children the importance of being kind to everyone. Teach them many people are having a very hard time in life that they don't tell others about. Explain to them that there are many people who don't know Jesus, or come from nice homes like they have been blessed with. But they are still people with the same feelings we have and should be treated the same way we want to be treated. Teach them to think of others and when they want something or want to do something, to think about how it will this affect others. Will our actions make them happy or sad? Teach them that sometimes it's just good to put the other person and their feelings first. Teach them to do things for others, because we love Jesus and that is what He does.

Manners

> "The most effective way to raise a nice child
> is to be a nice adult"
> L.R. Knost

Our society today is greatly lacking in basic manners. This can only mean that they are not being taught in the home.

Teach your children to address elders as mister or missus, and their uncles and aunts as such, instead of calling them by their first name. This shows that they respect them. If we want our children to use manners and show respect to others, we have to as well. Lead by example. If they see us consistently showing respect to others and using manners, they will naturally do it too.

Teach children to be thankful.

A good game to play would be to see who could list the most things they are thankful for. This will produce a thankful heart in your children.

Teach children respect for authority. If they see you respecting authority like their father, or the police, they will too. Again, lead by example.

Integrity

The merriam-webster.com dictionary defines integrity as: trustworthiness and incorruptibility to a degree that one is incapable of being false to a trust, responsibility, or pledge.

The best way to teach personal integrity is like most things, by example. When your children see that you practice personal integrity in all your dealings, they are more likely to follow your example. My father's parents had a reputation of exceptional honesty, and they taught their children the importance of uncompromising honesty too. My father also taught us, his children, by word and deed the importance of honesty in every area of our lives. When he said something, you could count on the fact that he would do it. His word was his bond. He believed in doing an honest day's work and doing right by everyone he dealt with. When I became an adult and had children of my own it was up to me to instill this same training in my children. When a friend once remarked, "I can't believe that your children never lie," I knew that I had succeeded.

Personal integrity is a very important God-honoring trait to have. Since our Heavenly Father cannot lie; *It is impossible for God to lie* (Hebrews 6:18), and the enemy of our soul cannot tell the truth; *There is no truth in him* (John 8:44), it is very important for us to strive to be like our Heavenly Father and be people of honesty. Whatever good you teach your children, teach them the importance of being honest in all they do. This will make an enormous difference in their life. Teach them it is never right to do wrong, and doing right because it's right won't always be popular but it will make their life better, giving them a clear conscience and pleasing their Heavenly Father. Teach them to always listen for their inner voice that whispers to their heart. It will tell them what is right and what is wrong. Teach them that not listening to our inner voice and obeying it is much like not wearing our seatbelt. The first time we don't wear our seatbelt and the buzzer goes off, it sounds so loud that it startles us. But the more we ignore that buzzer and don't wear our seatbelt, in our mind the noise from the buzzer gets softer and softer until we are finally able to tune it out completely. Then if we happen to be in a car accident, we may learn the hard way that we should have listened to that buzzer and put the seatbelt on because it is there to keep us safe. Our inner voice is much like that. It is put there by God to keep us safe but it is up to us to choose to listen and obey it.

Teaching your children the importance of listening to their inner voice will keep them out of a lot of trouble. Tell them they can recognize their inner voice is telling them not to do something by the uneasy, prickly, heavy feeling they feel on the inside of them. It's trying to tell them what they are about to do is wrong.

Asking for Forgiveness

As parents, we all make mistakes with our children at one time or another. We sometimes get angry and lose our temper, or we may say things that hurt them or even do things that set the wrong example. When we do, we must go to God and repent, and then also ask our children to forgive us. This will teach them that when they do or say something they shouldn't, they can go to God and ask for and receive forgiveness and then come to us or whomever they've wronged and also ask for and receive forgiveness. Then it should not be brought up again.

Teach your children how to ask for forgiveness from those they may have hurt by their words or deeds. Do some practicing. This will help them know what to do if they are in that situation.

How to sincerely ask for forgiveness when you hurt someone:
1. Go to them and tell them what you did.
2. Admit you were wrong.
3. Tell them you are sorry and ask them to forgive you.
4. Lastly, tell them to the best of your ability you will never do it again.

Tell your children, "We are just practicing now, but when you do this for real, it has to be sincere and from your heart."

Let them know how very important it is to go to Jesus and the people they have wronged right away and ask for forgiveness, otherwise they will feel shame over what they have done and that will make them want to avoid saying their prayers and avoid the person they have hurt. Saying, "I'm sorry," is very important to teach our children. There are many adults and children who refuse to say they are sorry or admit they have done anything wrong. This is really a bad attitude to have because it makes a person become hard-hearted. We want our children to always keep a tender heart toward us and other people, and most importantly toward the Lord.

Teaching

> "Instead of buying your children all the things you never had, teach them all the things you were never taught."
> Bruce Lee

Instructing our children is a full-time job, and we are always their teacher. This doesn't apply only to spiritual things, although they are the most important, it also applies to every area of life. *Instructing* is the key word here. Instructing until the job can be done and done well by the child that is learning it. It can take different amounts of time depending on the job and the child's ability to learn it. Some jobs are easier to learn than others. Be patient We must always keep in mind that they are children, not adults.

> "It's not what you do for your children,
> but what you have taught them to do for
> themselves, that will make them successful
> human beings."
> Ann Landers

When I worked in the factory, I learned an excellent way of teaching a job in four easy steps. It will work for any job and for any age. Making sure they have thoroughly learned each step before moving on to the next is the key to their success. Each step may take a few sessions for your child to learn.

1. First do the job yourself start to finish, with your child watching you do it. Do it slow enough so that you can show them every step thoroughly, explaining it to them as you go.
2. Next, have your child do the job with you, still training as you go.
3. Then when that is accomplished and you feel like they are ready, have them do the job by themselves, with you watching.
4. Finally, when they are fully trained and can do the job well on their own, show them that you trust them to do the job well by having them do the job by themselves without you there watching them.

Encourage them by telling them how well they are learning the job. If they make a mistake, be patient with them. Tell them it's ok and that they will do better next time. Then, when they have fully learned the job, tell them how well they have learned it and how proud you are of them.

This is actually a good pattern for training anything you want them to learn. Once your children completely master the job and you heartily praise them for it, their self-confidence will grow and they will become more self-reliant. A win for both of you.

It's never too early to start teaching them life skills that will help them all through their life. Delegate jobs to your children by their ability to learn not necessarily by their age.

Teach them to respect their home by taking good care of it and to be proud of how it looks. Also it is good to teach them to work for some of what they get, for then they will value it more, and this also teaches them responsibility. Teach them how to take good care of their own things.

Continually teach them in all the aspects of life. This will be more time-consuming, but it will pay big dividends when they learn how to do things on their own. Remember, when you teach them to do things for themselves, this will become one less thing you will have to do for them, and they will be learning important life skills. As they learn how to do jobs around the house and take responsibility for certain tasks, you will be able to spend more time with them doing things you both enjoy.

As you teach your children, don't expect perfection, but work toward it. If what they do is never good enough for you, it will cause them to get discouraged and this can chip away at their self-confidence. We must always work to build their confidence in themselves, not destroy it.

I remember seeing my sister-in-law sitting on the floor in the kitchen of their home with her young daughter cleaning and polishing the front of their refrigerator. She was in no hurry but just talked her through it very patiently. That same daughter of hers is now an adult and very at home in the kitchen doing whatever needs to be done. She has been trained well and is very self-reliant. In fact, she did this with all of her children in every area of their lives. Because she took the time to do this, they are all very self-reliant. They have been trained well and will do well in life.

Job Success

There will be times when your children get discouraged trying to learn a job they feel is just too hard for them to do. That's when you must set them up for success by giving them something else to do you know they will be able to do well, and then praising them for it. You can always go back to the harder job at another time and work with them to help them conquer it.

Always be their cheerleader. Inspire them and tell them repeatedly they can do anything if they just try. Confidence in any area can be built in a child when we train them well and then tell them how well they are doing. Once they're fully trained, let them know you trust them to do the jobs at home without watching over their shoulder. This will teach them to be self-reliant, and this is a very important quality to have if we want them be successful in life.

When you see them doing what they are supposed to do without being reminded, let them know that you notice it. This will encourage them to do it again. Always try to make them feel good about doing the right thing; everyone loves praise. However, it's not good to overly praise them for doing what they're supposed to do because this will set them up to feel they must always be praised for everything they do.

Let's take a look at some jobs around the house that children can do.

The main goal in learning jobs around the house is to give children confidence in themselves and teach them life skills they will need in their adult life. Teach them everything they need to know to run a home efficiently. Then with the knowledge they have learned at home, they will have the confidence they need to start their adult life fully prepared.

When children are taught early on that household jobs, inside and out, are everyone's responsibility, you won't have the battle of trying to get them to help when they get older. They will do what is required automatically and without resentment.

"Children become irresponsible only when we fail to give them the opportunity to be responsible."
Unknown Author

A few years ago we went to visit my brother and his family. Neither he nor my sister-in-law were home at that time, but we were greeted at the door by their sixteen-year-old daughter. She welcomed us and asked us in, took our coats, and invited us into the kitchen. Next, she asked us to sit down and offered us some refreshments. Then, she sat down and talked to us just like an adult. They obviously did a good job training her.

Cleaning

Get your children involved in the cleaning process. Even a two-year-old can pick up their toys, put them where they belong, and also put their dirty clothes in the hamper. Children can often do far more for themselves than we think they can. The family motto here is "everyone likes to live in a clean house, so everyone helps keep it clean."

Cooking

When a child is young, they can start learning how to do things to help prepare a meal. Even smaller children can get some potatoes and bring them to the older child who will be peeling them.

Draw a pattern on an index card for setting the table. This will help them learn to set the table correctly on their own. Then, praise them for doing such a good job.

Teach them to bake and to cook. If they choose a meal that they like and help you prepare it, they will eat better because they had a hand in choosing and preparing the food themselves. The family motto here is "everyone likes to eat, so everyone helps prepare the food."

Laundry

Teach your children to always put their dirty clothes in the hamper. When they get a little older they can learn how to sort, wash, fold neatly, and put away the laundry. Even small children can match socks. The family motto here is "everyone likes clean clothes, so everyone helps do the laundry."

Sometimes, as they are helping you with the work around the house, it would be good to tell them, when the work is done they can have some ice cream or do something they want to do, or that you will do something with them they would like. This will give them a goal with a reward to work toward, and it will make the job more pleasant for them.

Don't let them think the work at home is never done. As mothers, we often feel that way, but it isn't good for children to think all there is at home is work.

Jobs for Hire

Post a few "for hire" jobs on a bulletin board with different rewards listed for each job well done

Have some jobs "required" and some jobs "for hire." When they get their required jobs done, tell them they will be able to do a "for hire" job and make a little extra money or get a special privilege they want.

Dusting for dimes is a great way to get the dusting done and give your children some incentive for helping. Tell them how many there are and make some a little difficult to find. If they are having difficulty finding them, play the game of "you're getting warmer" when they're getting closer to them, and "you're getting colder" when they're getting farther away from them. This will help guide them so they can find all the dimes. This way you will get a good dusting job done and they will have fun doing it. It's a win for both you and your children.

Jars

Make a couple of jars and label them. One could be the "Treat Jar," and one could be the "Job Jar." To each jar add slips of different colored paper, one color for each child. Write what the treat or job will be on these slips of paper. Then fold them so that what is written on them can't be seen and put them in the jar. Have them reach in and get a slip of paper that is their color, then open it and read what it says.

Treat Jar

These treats could be a reward for learning an especially hard task or putting extra effort toward doing a really good job. They could be anything you can think of that each child would like, such as a small toy they've been wanting to get, a game they would like to play, some place they want to go, or maybe even a little money. You'll know just what kind of treat each of your children would like to have.

This is not to be used when they do their assigned jobs. Your own discretion will guide you to know when it is appropriate.

Job Jar

This jar is for extra chores to be used as punishment for disobedience. These jobs could be extra work around the house or doing something for an elderly neighbor. Even with this, now and then, slip in a mercy pass for each child. Here would be a good place to teach them what mercy really is. Explain to them why we are given mercy from God even though punishment is deserved.

God's Protective Fence

What a wonderful thing to know that God has promised that He will always protect us.

The angel of the Lord encamps around those who
fear him, and he delivers them.
Psalm 34:7

As the mountains surround Jerusalem, so the Lord
surrounds his people both now and forevermore.
Psalm 125:2

The reason Jesus tells us not to do certain things is because He knows these are the things that will hurt us in the long run. He doesn't want His children to be hurt any more than we want ours to be. He wants us to know that these rules are not to fence us in but they are to create a protective fence that will protect us and keep trouble out.

To explain this to a young child, you could draw a picture of a yard with a fence around it and a road nearby. Draw a car on the road and some big bad animals out on the other side of the road. In the yard you could draw a puppy, with a doghouse and toys. Make sure there is lots of extra room for the puppy to run and play. Explain that as long as the puppy stays inside the protective fence he is safe; no wild animals or mean dogs can get in the protective fence to hurt him. But if he gets out of the protective fence, these bigger animals can hurt him, or he might run into the road and get hit by a car. Tell them how much safer the puppy is if he stays inside the protective fence where he has lots of room to run and play with all of his toys. He doesn't see the danger outside the fence, but you do, and you know that inside the protective fence the puppy is safe, but outside he could easily get hurt. Then, explain this is the reason there are rules. God's rules and your rules are the protective fence that keeps bad things out and keeps them protected from getting hurt.

For an older child you could use the example of someone they know who had started smoking when they were a teenager and now have cancer from it, or someone who tried a little drugs to join in with their friends and is now hooked on them, and all the problems they are having because of their addiction. These people have stepped out of God's protective fence and off the path that God has chosen for them. They are doing things God does not want them to do.

Diligently teach your children the things that will help them understand why God tells them not to do certain things. He knows these are the things that will hurt them one way or another and He wants to keep them from getting hurt. It may look like fun things are happening on the other side of that protective fence, but in the long run these very things will eventually result in heartache, pain, and a lifetime of regret.

Choosing a Path for Life

> *Children are a heritage from the Lord,*
> *offspring a reward from him.*
> *Like arrows in the hands of a warrior*
> *are children born in one's youth.*
> Psalm 127: 3-5

Our children are the arrows that God has given us, and it is up to us to be the warrior who will skillfully guide them to reach the right target, the target that will please God, and give them a happy life.

There is a destination to every path in life.

There may be times when we see their actions don't line up with the direction that will lead them to a good life. Then, it is up to us to lovingly, and skillfully, guide them back to the right path and help them reach the right destination.

If you see them making the wrong decisions and veering off the good path, sit down with them, lovingly put your arm around them, tell them what the end results will be if they keep doing what they are doing, and ask them if this is what they want their life to be like. Tell them about some other people who have stayed on the same path they are on and have ruined their life and even the lives of others.

It is imperative, and I do mean imperative, that we let our children know that if they decide to take a certain path and they find out it is leading them to a place they don't want to go and know they shouldn't be on, they need to get off that path as soon as possible and get back on the right path. Let them know that *u-turns are always possible,* and that you will always be there to help them get back on the right path, no matter what.

My dear children, I write this to you so that you will not sin. But if anybody does sin, we have an advocate with the Father—Jesus Christ, the Righteous One
1 John 2:1

Diligently teach your children that at the beginning of every path there is a crossroad with two different paths to choose from. One path leads to a good destination, and here the Lord has carefully chosen the best path for us, where there will be peace, joy, and good things that follow. *I have come that they may have life, and have it to the full* (John 10:10). The other path leads to a bad destination. Here the devil has also carefully chosen a path for us, but this path will lead us to untold heartache, pain, and regret. *The thief* [devil] *comes only to steal and to kill, and to destro*y (John 10:10). The *only* reason he comes to us, is to steal, kill or destroy something that we hold precious in our life. It could be our health or even our relationships with those we love the most.

The devil flaunts the bait, but hides the hook.

I heard this statement a long time ago. It says so clearly what the enemy has planned for us. I've never forgotten it because it's so very true. How many times do we hear a person say when they get into trouble, "It looked so innocent, I never dreamed it would end up this way." The bad path leads us to a certain amount of fun at first to get us hooked, but later on, the bad consequences will surely happen, and they will be even worse than we ever imagined. There are many things that may look good to us, but God sees the big picture and can see that in the long run, these things will harm us in one way or the another.

The beginning of the good path usually doesn't look as fun or intriguing as the bad path may look, but the good path leads to good things happening now and even better things later on. However, if we choose a path that God has warned us against, it will often lead us to a place we have no intention of going.

The Law of Unintended Consequences

It's important for adults and children alike to realize that when we choose a certain behavior, we automatically choose the consequences that go along with it. With every decision we make there are hidden consequences that follow, good or bad. We don't usually see these hidden consequences until after we have done the deed. This is called "the law of unintended consequences." God already knows the consequences for each decision, and He doesn't want us to go against His laws because He doesn't want us to suffer the bad consequences that automatically go along with disobedience.

The Lord loves us, and He knows where each path leads and if it will bring us happiness and a good life or if it will bring heartache and a life filled with sorrow and regret. He wants us to choose the good path for our sakes not His. There is a very good reason the Lord wants us to stay on the path that He has laid out for us. That is because this path has a built-in hedge that will stand guard between us and a lot of life's heartaches. On this path we'll have a life of peace of heart and mind. God's favor is upon this path, and He has placed more blessings along it than we can even imagine. This doesn't mean we will have a trouble-free life, but it does mean that nothing will touch us that hasn't already been screened by Him.

It is up to us as parents to guide our children, like arrows being shot at a target, to choose the right path. It's the choices they make now that will make all the difference in the quality of their life later on. Regret is a hard thing to live with.

Decisions

When our granddaughter was young, our daughter-in-law played what she called the "common sense game" with her. She would make up a situation and ask her daughter what she should do if she was in that situation. When our granddaughter said what she thought she should do, her mother would tell her what the results of that decision would be. If there was a better way of handling the situation she would tell her what the better decision was and then what the results of the better decision would be. She would then ask her which of the two results she would rather have. Of course, she would choose the result from the better decision. This taught her to think seriously about every decision she made because they automatically had either a good or bad consequence that came along with them.

This is a great way to teach children how to make good decisions for themselves. It will give them some forethought about many situations, and in their mind they will already know what to do or how to react.

There are two ways to learn which choices to make in life: the easy way and the hard way. The easy way is learning by example, that is, by watching what choices others have made, seeing the results they have gotten from their choices, good or bad, and following or avoiding their example. Learning the hard way is by experience, that is, by making our own choices, and experiencing the results of those actions. Choose the easy way.

Once you see that your children are capable of making good decisions, start allowing them to make some decisions for themselves, this will build up their confidence. They will sometimes learn to make good decisions by getting the results of making bad ones. As parents we hate to see this happen and we want to shield them from these results. But sadly, if they are never allowed to make the wrong decisions for themselves, they will not know how to make the right ones. How much better it is for them to learn little by little in the safety of a loving home with their parents to help guide them, than to never be allowed to make their own decision and then as adults be out in the cold, cruel world without the safety net of a loving family to help them. It's our responsibility to teach them how to make good decisions they will be happy with once they have made them.

Rules

Our whole life long there will always be rules we have to follow. God's rules, our parent's rules, our employer's rules, and our government's rules.

God's rules are the same for everyone, and our rules are what we think is appropriate behavior for each age group. We decide what is acceptable, and what is not. If something brings punishment one time but not the next or with one child and not the other, children won't know which behavior is acceptable and which one is not, so be consistent. Make the rules clear so everyone understands them. The right behavior and obeying the rules brings their own rewards, installing a pattern of integrity that will last a lifetime.

> "Children need the boundaries of discipline
> to protect them from a world they are not
> ready for."
> Sletrakor

We dearly love our children, so we must teach them to obey us, but we must also let them know we don't make rules because we want to keep them from having fun. Explain that your rules are made out of your love for them. They are there to protect them, and keep them out of trouble or danger, and to teach them how to live a successful, honorable life. You have lived a lot longer than they have and you know if they obey what you say, they will have a much better life. If children learn early on that their life will be much better when they obey your rules, it will be much easier for them to obey God's rules, which are also made out of His love for them. His rules are also to keep them out of trouble and to protect them from danger, which will give them a better life.

Rules without relationship create rebellion.

Talk to them about each of the rules you have for them. Then explain why each rule is necessary, what will happen if they follow your rules and what will happen if they don't. Then, they will realize the rules are there to help them, and they will understand that each rule is made out of our love for them, to protect them from harm. If we don't do this they may grow up with the idea that we make the rules just to boss them around with the attitude of "because I said so!"

When you need to talk seriously to them about something, sit down with them and put your arm lovingly around them, and then explain what you need to with a soft and tender voice.

Discipline

> Ignorance needs instruction,
> rebellion needs correction.

There are two different kinds of wrongdoing. The first thing we must do when we find that discipline is needed is to find out which kind of wrongdoing has been done. One is done because they don't fully understand what they are supposed to do or how to do it, the other is done out of rebellion because they don't want to do what they are told to do.

Before we punish, we should ask ourselves if we took the time to train them well in this area. Were we clear with our instructions? Sometimes our children just need better instructions rather than discipline. Then again, we can sometimes expect too much from our children. We must always remember that they are children, so they don't think like we do and don't have the experience we have to perform tasks.

Then there is another kind of wrongdoing, it is intentional disobedience out of rebellion. This kind of wrongdoing does indeed need discipline. Even with this, we must discipline according to their actions.

> "Make the punishment fit the crime."
> W. S. Gillbert

Discipline when it's needed, but don't discipline out of anger, cool down first. We are more likely to discipline far greater than their misdeeds deserved if we do it out of anger. Instead of yelling, use a firm but soft "I mean business" tone when correcting them.

When you have to punish your children, be careful you don't say hurtful things to them or about them. Never say things like "you'll never amount to anything" or "why can't you be like your brother he would never do this." These hurtful words can wound them far more, and stay with them longer than any other kind of punishment.

When we do have to correct them, we should show them in the Bible what God says about disobeying.

In Ephesians we find some scriptures that have important information for children. These scriptures tell of two promises from God that are a reward for them if they obey us:

Children, obey your parents in the Lord, for this is right. Honor your father and mother which is the first commandment with a promise. [Here is the first promise;] *so that it may go well with you,* [and here is the second promise;] *and that you may enjoy long life on the earth.*
Ephesians 6:1-3

I would say these rewards far outweigh the pleasure of disobedience, wouldn't you?

Caught

Not taking care of a problem soon after it arises will let roots of disobedience and rebellion start to get a foothold. This is something we definitely do not want to happen.

Ecclesiastes 8:11 warns us, *When the sentence for a crime is not quickly carried out, people's hearts are filled with schemes to do wrong.*

When children do wrong, the best thing for them is to get caught and corrected. Like driving a car, we must constantly make small adjustments to stay in the center of our lane. Correcting our children as soon as small misdeeds are done, not in anger but with a bit of an authoritative voice, will more likely keep them from larger acts of disobedience. Often if we tell our children *not* to do something, it's very likely this will be the one thing they will be drawn to do. Re-word what you want them to do, and tell them what *to* do, instead of what *not* to do.

Children who aren't taught accountability for their actions grow up to become adults who think nothing they do is wrong. Punishment for bad behavior shows them there are consequences that go along with not obeying the rules. If we explain why we want them to do what we ask and what will happen if they don't, they will be more willing to do the right thing.

Bad behavior, especially anger, can be controlled, but if we don't teach them to keep these things in check, they can start controlling them, giving them a hard heart.

The proper attitude toward a child's disobedience is this: "I love you too much to allow you to keep acting like this."

After the punishment is over, gently put your arm around your child and tell them you love them. Tell them they are starting down the wrong path and that you love them too much to let them continue to stay on that path of acting badly. If they stay on that path some kind of harm will eventually come to them. This will teach them that even though they have made a wrong choice, they are still loved. It doesn't make them bad. They are still a good boy or girl, they just need to make better choices. Yes, they should be corrected when they do wrong, but let that be done and over with. Then say good things to them, "You may have done so and so, and that was wrong, but I know you won't do that again. I had to correct you because I love you too much to let you continue to act like this."

Don't ever send your children to bed or to school feeling unloved. Get things resolved first and assure them they are very much loved.

Spoil

Although children need to know they are loved and an important part of the family, it will hurt them in the long run if they are given the impression they are the center of attention or that life revolves around them.

It is so easy to spoil our children without even realizing it because we naturally want to do good things for them. We want them to have the very best we can give them. But spoiling our children is one of the worst things we can do to them. Sadly, if this is overdone it will eventually lead to giving them a feeling of entitlement. A child that is catered to will become a demanding child. We must not let this happen. Our goal is to have a home of peace, and this is one very important part of creating a peaceful home. Diligence is crucial in this area.

I have seen countless examples of this and you will too if you just look around. Children, usually boys, who have mothers that would do anything to keep them from paying the price for doing wrong and giving them everything they want, become adults that won't work because they know that mom or someone will always pay their bills and keep food on their table. The child becomes an invalid in many ways and the mother becomes a slave. How very sad for both mother and child.

There will be times, especially when we're busy, rushed, or just plain tired, and they are persistent, that it will be easy to give in and let them do what they want, whether it's good for them or not. To their own hurt they will have found that persistent demanding to get their own way works. They will learn to be manipulative and will become difficult to get along with. They will expect preferential treatment from every other person all their life. This will lead them to become selfish and self-centered.

Undisciplined children become undisciplined teenagers and then uncaring and self-centered undisciplined adults. As adults, they will develop into poor employees, making it hard for them to keep a job. They will become inconsiderate, selfish, and demanding husbands or wives and will more likely turn to alcohol or drugs because they always want that feeling of superiority it gives them. An undisciplined child will develop the attitude that they are the only one that really matters, and they are the one in charge of every situation that comes up.

One thing we must always remember is that we are raising someone's husband or wife and our grandchildren's fathers and mothers. This is an awesome responsibility.

School

Help your children prepare their lunches and put their next day's school clothes out the night before. This will save a lot of time in the morning. Of course, when they are very young, you'll have to do most of this yourself, but as they grow older they will have learned how to do this for themselves.

On days when you know they will have something especially difficult to do, put an extra treat in their lunch, or write them a little note with a few words of encouragement, like, "I know you'll do good on your test today," or, "I'm making your favorite dessert for supper tonight." This will encourage them and let them know you are thinking about them.

Don't overload them with activities outside the home, let them choose one or two school activities to join.

When we send our children off to school in the morning remember that harsh, stinging words will rob them of productivity all day, but kind, loving words will encourage them and help them in their studies.

Friends

> *Do not be misled:*
> *Bad company corrupts good character.*
> 1 Corinthians 15:33

Guide your children in picking their friends. Teach them to be very careful in choosing their close friends and even more careful choosing their best friends. Teach them what to look for in a friend. The very first requirement for a friend should be that they are a *true* Christian. God gives us these wise instructions in choosing a friend. *Do not be yoked together with unbelievers* (2 Corinthians 6:14). We don't hear much about yokes today, but many years ago, this was something used on oxen. When two of them were put together to pull things like carts or farm equipment, it would make sure they both were going in the same direction. The Merriam-Webster dictionary defines a yoke as: "A wooden bar or frame by which two draft animals (such as oxen) are joined at the heads or necks for working together." You can imagine what would happen, in this case if one oxen would pull one way and the other pulled the other way. That is an example of what happens when a Christian is put together with a non-Christian. They both want to follow different paths in life, which will naturally bring a lot of conflict to their relationship.

> Children are often drawn to people who act foolish because it looks like this person is having a lot of fun, and they naturally want to have fun too.

Teach your children it's important to surround themselves with people they want to be like because they will become like those they choose for their friends, good or bad. Proverbs 13:20 tells us we have two choices for choosing friends. Our first choice is to *walk with the wise and become wise,* [our second choice is], *for a companion of fools suffers harm.* Here the Bible states that over a period of time, by association we become like those we associate with. First it states that if we walk with those who are wise, we will, by association, become wise. The second choice is the companion of fools that suffers harm. They suffer harm because, by association, they will learn the ways of a fool, and these ways sooner or later will produce harm. Oh, the fool will no doubt suffer harm from their own actions too, but here the Bible is warning the one who innocently becomes friends with a fool and suffers harm because of it.

Choosing a church that has a strong youth group and a leader that closely follows God will be a big help keeping your children on the right path because they will most likely choose their friends from their church group who will be a good influence on them and help them stand strong for Jesus. Also, they will be taught important instructions from the Bible that will give them a firm foundation in following Christ.

Explain to them the things show that a person is a true friend, and also what shows they are not. Tell them if your friend is telling you something they promised another friend they wouldn't tell anyone, be assured they will tell others anything you tell them in confidence too. If they talk bad about other friends behind their back, they will do the same to you. Teach them to be the one who does the choosing of their friends, and don't just leave it to anyone who befriends them. As parents, it is extremely important to keep your eyes wide open to this because the wrong friends can lead your children down the wrong path that could ultimately ruin their lives. I've seen this happen many times. Remember what 1 Corinthians 15:33 warns us, *Do not be misled: Bad company corrupts good character.*

Teenager Music

As your children get older and become teenagers, music will become a big part of their life, just like it did for us at that age. Do some research, ask other parents who have successfully raised teens that live for Christ or the youth leader at your church to help you find music that sends a message that encourages them to follow Christ. The most important thing is the words that are sung, not the music that is played. Make sure the words in the songs are words you want your teenagers to have in their minds, because the songs we listen to will often repeat over and over in our mind, and these words can have a big influence, good or bad. Today there is a lot of good contemporary Christian music they will enjoy, and that will be exactly what you want your children to listen to and having running over and over, like songs do, in their minds.

Dress

Dressing well is for the whole family. This doesn't mean they need a lot of clothes, just that they need the right clothes for everything they do; school, church, and play. See the section on dressing the family, in Chapter 1.

We should dress our children the best we can with clean stylish clothes that look good. Having up-to-date things to wear will help them feel good about themselves and boost their self-confidence. Peer pressure is often harder on children than it is on adults. Always keep in mind they don't want to stand out, they want to fit in. Teach them how to put an outfit together, and how to match colors and styles.

Because girls are more clothes conscious than boys are, we can easily spend more time and money on dressing our daughters nice and stylish and forget that even though our sons are not as clothes conscious as our daughters, they want to be dressed nice too. So we must see to it that each one of them has the clothes they need to dress well.

With our daughters, we must teach them that modesty is very important and to always remember that men and boys are visual. A girl that dresses immodestly will catch their eye in the wrong way. We don't want to give the enemy a chance to put improper thoughts in the minds of these men and boys or put our daughters in danger. So this means we must make sure our daughters dress modestly, not only for their protection, but also to please God. They can still dress stylish, just add a layer or two for modesty. If the skirt is too short, add some capri leggings. If the blouse is too low, add a camisole that comes up higher under it.

When I was growing up we always wore dresses to school and church. Because my mother wanted to instill a habit of modesty in us, she repeatedly told my sister and me to always be "lady like", and when you're sitting down she would say, "Keep your knees and ankles together."

Daughters

If you act like a lady, you'll be treated like a lady.

I was told this many times as a teenager, and I've found over the years that it is very good advice because it's so true. Teach your daughters how to walk, talk, and conduct themselves like a lady.

Pretty is as pretty does.

Pretty is only skin deep. The most important beauty, true beauty, is the kind that comes from the inside from a kind and loving spirit. A pretty face may get a guy interested in a date, but a kind and loving spirit is what a man of quality looks for in a date or a wife.

While they are still young, it would be wise to start teaching your daughters how to be good wives and mothers because that is their future. Teach them how to take good care of their appearance and their belongings. Teach them how to plan a menu and to make good nutritious meals. As we've often said, for that the best way to teach anything is to model it yourself. Our daughters may be career motivated, but they still need to know how to conduct themselves as women.

Teach your daughters to let their date open doors for them, help them with their coat, and leave it to him to be the leader. This will be interpreted by him as respect, and respect is very important to a young man. When deciding what to do on their date, unless something else is really important to them, they should let their date decide what to do. If he's a young man of quality, he will make decisions based on pleasing your daughter. But if he decides to do something she knows is wrong, she should insist he take her home, or she should immediately call her parents to come and get her.

There will be times when a young man she doesn't want to go out with will ask her to go on a date with him. It's important to prepare her so she knows ahead of time how to handle this situation. Teach her how to graciously decline the date. Remembering that it takes a lot of courage for a young man to ask a girl out on a date and that a young man's confidence is very fragile at this time in his life. Write out a dialogue and practice it with her so she will know how to graciously and kindly decline the date without making him feel rejected.

A few suggestions in turning down a date.
1. Thank him for asking, but don't give him false hope.
2. Put a negative between two positives, sandwich style.
3. Thank you for your offer, I'm flattered you asked.
4. You seem like a really good person, but I don't think we are right for each other.
5. I've been known for not recognizing a good thing when I'm faced with it. This is a compliment with the message of, no.
6. Put yourself in his shoes and think about how you would feel.
7. Treat him the way you would want to be treated.

Sons

Teach your sons how to be good husbands and fathers because this is what they will one day be. It's good for sons also to be taught how to take care of a home and family. A lot of things have to be taught to your sons by their father, but there are some things you can teach them since you are well aware of how a young lady wants to be treated.

It's important to teach your sons to be gentlemen and to treat girls with respect. Teach them how to pay compliments, and how to help a girl put her coat on and how to help her take it off, how to open doors for her and stand back so she can walk in first, how to open the car door for her and wait until she is safely inside then to close the door for her. When he is walking down a street with a young lady he should always walk on the side closest to the road to shield her from anything that could harm her. This makes a girl feel cared for.

When your son grows into a young man he will still need your love but not the smothering kind. Even a young man, needs to be shown respect.

Sons and Daughters

Hold yourself to a high standard, you won't be sorry.
Be the kind of person you want to attract.
Value yourself because you are valuable.
Set a high standard for what kind of behavior is acceptable to you in a date or a friend, and stick to it.

Learn to stand up for yourself in the right way.

Always remember that what you allow will continue. Pause and think about this. It's very important.

Don't settle for someone who is just ok just to be with someone.

Girls, don't let them take away from you what they can never give back.

Sticking to these things shows the person that our Sons and daughters date, that they expect to be shown respect and treated well, and they won't settle for anything less.

Mate

> "Don't marry the person you think you can live with: marry only the one you know you can't live without."
> James C. Dobson

When your children become teenagers it's a good idea to start teaching them what to look for in a God-honoring date, which could eventually lead to be a God-honoring mate. Point out different people as examples and what kind of mate they have chosen. Tell them how it affected their life and the life of their children. Show them people who have made good choices and also those who have made poor choices.

In looking for a mate, there's a chance that even if they come from a good Christian family they could turn out bad, but it is much less likely. This is why our children need God's guidance to help them see the real person. Anyone can be a kind and honorable person for a while, but sooner or later their true self will be shown, either good or bad. So encourage them to take their time choosing the person they will spend the rest of their life with. Help them to seek God's choice for them. He knows who will be their perfect match and He knows their true heart. God will help them see the real person if they ask Him to.

Teach your children that the most important decision they will ever make is choosing to live for Jesus. The second-most important decision that they will ever make is choosing their life's mate. This choice will make all the rest of their life either good or bad, and it will also make all the difference in the life of their future children. We've learned how to choose our friends, but choosing the right mate to spend a lifetime with is far more important. Like we talked about with choosing our friends, the same forewarning is amplified of not being, *yoked together with unbelievers,* (2 Corinthians 6:14). This is much more important when choosing someone to spend the rest of their life with. They say that opposites attract, and that is true, but the problem with that is they don't get along good for any length of time. Soon problems will undoubtedly arise in the relationship because they are both pulling in different directions, each one wanting a different way of life.

When God was bringing the children of Israel into the land He had promised them, they first had to drive out the ungodly idol worshipers who were there. He gave them this mandate. *Do not intermarry with them. Do not give your daughters to their sons or take their daughters for your sons,* [and then He gave them the reason for this mandate], *for they will turn your children away from following me to serve other gods* (Deuteronomy 7:3-4). God gives the same mandate to us today because He knows the same thing could happen to our children if they intermarry with an unbeliever. In 1 Kings 3:7-12 we find an example of this. Here we read of a conversation between King Solomon and God. When King Solomon first came to the throne, he asked God to give him an understanding heart to rule the people, and because he didn't ask for things to please himself, God answered his request. He said, *I will give you a wise and discerning heart, so that there will never have been anyone like you, nor will there ever be.* So, King Solomon became the wisest man that ever lived, yet later on in (1 Kings 11:1-4) we read that he chose many idol worshiping women to be his wives, who eventually turned his heart away from the one true God he had lived for all his life, to the useless god's that his wives worshiped.

A minister was counseling a young woman on her choice of a boyfriend. The young woman said, "I know that I really shouldn't be dating this unsaved young man, but I feel like I can win him to Christ." The minister wisely told her that, "Most likely the young man will have a greater influence on you than you will have on him." But she still insisted that he was wrong, so the minister proceeded to give her a little lesson she would never forget. He had her climb up on a chair and try to pull him up to where she was standing. She took his hand and tried and tried to no avail. Next, the minister took hold of her hand and gave her a little jerk, and down she came with one pull. Then he told her, "It is much easier for an unsaved boyfriend to drag down a Christian girlfriend than it is for a Christian girlfriend to win an unsaved boyfriend to Christ." Point out some people who are examples of this to your children. Sadly, they are everywhere.

Only God can change someone, and even then, that person has to be willing to admit they were wrong and ask God to help them. We have a hard enough time changing our own self when we need to, how can we change anyone else?

When our children are considering someone for more than just a casual date, it is important for them to take a good look at the family their date comes from. How does their father treat their mother? How does their mother treat their father? This will usually be a good indicator of how they will be treated if they were to marry this person.

For our sons, intently watch to see how the girl's mother treats her father. This girl will most likely treat her husband the same way.

For our daughters, intently watch to see how the boy's father treats his mother. This boy will most likely treat his wife the same way.

Have your children answer these questions about the person they are thinking about marrying. They can keep the answers to themselves or tell them to you, you decide.

Keep your standard high for the person you choose.

> Tell them to be honest with themselves when they answer these questions about the person they are dating.
> First and foremost, are they a godly Christian, not just a Christian, but a truly godly Christian?
> Do they have the Fruit of the Spirit in their life which is, love, joy, peace, patience or an even temper, kindness, goodness or helpfulness to others, faithfulness, gentleness and self-control? (Galatians 5: 22-23)
> What are their core values?
> Are the honest in all they do?
> Do they respect authority?
> Are they teachable, or do they know it all?
> Are they good and faithful workers?
> Are they honest and trustworthy?
> Are they hotheaded, angry, or controlling?
> How do they treat people who can do nothing for them in return?
> How do they treat people who may be on a lower social scale than they are?

These are very important core values that need to be seriously considered when our children are choosing their life's mate.

Some more important questions they need to seriously think about are: Is this person the kind of person they want to be the parent to the precious children they will someday have? Are their parents the kind of people they want to be their precious children's grandparents? What kind of example will they be to their children? You see, your children are not just choosing a life's mate for themselves, they are also choosing the father, or mother, and grandparents for their future children. Instill in them the importance of choosing wisely.

Tell them if there are any red flags coming up in their heart to pay close attention to them and move on. This will save them from a lot of heartache and tears in the years to come.

Teach them they are too valuable to settle for someone they don't truly love, even if they are a good person. Encourage them to wait until God brings them that special person who will be perfect for them. Tell your children that God has the perfect person already picked out for them and He will bring them into their life at just the right time. When He does, they will know deep down in their heart they are the right one, and they'll have complete peace and no doubts about it.

Sometimes they may have to wait a while before God brings that special person into their life. But if they are willing to wait, they will be glad they did for all the rest of their life.

Handling Situations

Knowing how to handle situations before they happen and how to defuse them when necessary will help your children tremendously. Sooner or later they may have to deal with some of these situations. It will also help your children to understand why people act in unkind ways. This will by no means excuse that person for their bad behavior but it will help your child to understand why certain people act the way they do. Children should be taught not to give in to a person who demonstrates bad behavior.

Bullying

First of all, teach your children not to be a bully. A bully is often insecure and craves attention. A bully will usually pick on someone who is shy or a person who they know will not, or cannot, stand up for themselves. Children who stay mostly to themselves are often targets for bullies. The bully usually does his dirty work in front of an audience because they crave the attention they get, and they also like the feeling of superiority it gives them to pick on someone who is weaker than they are. But there are times a bully will get a child off to themselves and bully them. When they do this, they don't want anyone to know about it because they know they will get in trouble for what they are doing. Knowing their victim is afraid of them to start with, they threaten their victim with violence if they tell what the bully is doing to them. Teach your children not to give in to a bully and how to react to them if they are confronted by one.

1. Teach your child how to walk and carry themselves with confidence.
2. If you are anywhere near a bully, stay in a group of your friends as much as possible.
3. If they confront you, look them straight in the eye.
4. Never show signs of fear, as fear is the reaction they want.

Stalking

If someone is stalking them, teach them what to do to stop it or avoid it.

1. First and foremost, tell your family and friends, your teachers, or anyone you trust about what is happening.
2. Never go to a secluded place alone, keep someone else with you.
3. Never be alone with them.
4. Don't make eye contact with them.
5. Never talk to them. They are looking for attention from you, don't give it to them.
6. Do what you must do to avoid them.
7. Take pictures of them and their license plate number if they are in a car.
8 If they try to intimidate you, dial 911 and then hit send on your phone.
9. If you are driving and they are following you, don't go home. Go to a well populated area, never

a side street and blow your horn to draw attention to what is happening.
10. Don't fall for the "flat tire help" trick. If it really is flat, drive on the rim rather than put yourself in a position where they can take hold of you.

Attack

If someone tries to attack you

1. If at all possible, run away from them as fast as you can.
2. Scream as loud as you can.
3. Fight back and fight hard. Go for their soft flesh. Grab at their throat and grab hard to cut off their air supply. Gouge their eyes. Hit as hard as you can, and scratch them, especially their face to mark them.

In Conclusion

What an honor it will be when your children are grown, and you see that they are happy, responsible, and self-reliant adults. Then you will know you have taught them well, and as Proverbs 31:28 says, *Her children arise and call her blessed.*

Always remember that as a mother you're not only making memories for your children, you're making memories for yourself. You want these memories to be good ones for both of you. One day your children will be grown and gone. This is when those precious memories will fill your heart and mind. Be diligent now to do what will make those memories sweet.

With your children in mind, right now is the hardest, busiest, and happiest years of your life. So I'll say once again, it won't always be easy, but it will be absolutely worth it!

Chapter 4

The Guests of the House

Offer hospitality one to another
1 Peter 4:9

"Hospitality is simply an opportunity to show love."
Unknown Author

Having a Guest

In this chapter, we'll be looking at the ministry of hospitality. The Bible says we should practice hospitality. To practice means to keep working at something until we have perfected it.

If you know well in advance you have guests coming to visit, you can take the time to make special arrangements to suit their taste in food and what they like to do for activities. If they have small children, have some games, toys, movies, and storybooks suited for their age. Making the visit pleasant for them and their family will make them feel special and they will know they are important to you.

> When your adult children and their families come to visit, they should be at the very top of your list of people to treat well.

If you pay attention, keep your ears open, and watch people, you will learn what their likes and dislikes are. I keep a list in my household notebook just for this. I list each family and close friend. For each family, I list the husband, wife and every child with their birthdays and anniversaries listed. When I hear them say they like or don't like something, I write it down. I listen for them to mention their favorite meal, dessert, candy, color, what they like to read, or anything they especially like or don't like. Sometimes I ask questions about their preferences. If you do this, when it comes time for a visit or a gift you'll be well prepared to please your guest or the recipient of a gift.

> "In its essence, a meal is a creative act that has its genesis in the end of someone who cares enough to plan it, gather the ingredient and labor over its creation."
> Andi Ashworth

Say that you have a guest coming to your home and you know they love roast beef and lemon pie, and they don't like peas or blueberries. You make sure that roast beef is on the menu and peas are not. Then you have lemon pie for dessert, not something with blueberries in it. If they have any dietary restrictions keep them in mind and build your meal around it when planning your meal. Don't forget to take into consideration what food their children like or don't like.

There is also something else important to consider. Say your husband or one of your children doesn't like anything lemon. Because your precious family is more important than anyone else in your life, you would make sure there is something else they really enjoy for dessert. Now you've made everyone feel special.

Maybe they really like to play a certain game. Make sure you have it and know how to play it. After dinner, you might suggest you play the game that they love. Doing these things will let them know, without saying a word, how glad you are they are there.

If they are staying overnight, make sure to have fresh sheets and bedding on the bed for them and that their room is fresh and clean. Add some extra blankets or an afghan, a couple of extra pillows, and a place for their suitcase to sit, a box of tissue, and an alarm clock.

Some other things that will make them feel comfortable and cared for would be to put some bottled water or a tray with a pretty pitcher of water and a glass turned upside down on a napkin. Some paper, and pens, individually wrapped candy, granola bars, or some fruit, and of course a few chocolates are always welcome as well. Top it off with a few magazines or books that fit their taste, and they'll think they're being catered to in a high-end hotel.

Their bathroom should be clean and have fresh towels, washcloths, and a new bar of soap just for them. Put a basket in the bathroom with a few extra toothbrushes, some travel-size shampoo, toothpaste, mouthwash, and a shower hat just in case they forgot to bring one. Also, make sure you have a few night lights so no one stumbles in the dark.

Don't do a lot of bragging on the great things that are happening in your life or that of your family. People will be happy for you, but they will think more of you if you applaud what good things are happening in their life and their family. Making them feel loved and encouraged should be our main goal with guests.

Don't gossip. This is not only bad manners but more importantly it is displeasing to God. Matthew 7:1-2 warns us, *Do not judge, or you too will be judged. For in the same way you judge others, you will be judged.*

Try and keep the conversation on a positive level. Everyone has troubles in life, but if the conversation turns negative, change the subject as soon as possible, for if it goes on and on, it will ruin the visit. If you see they want some advice, try to give them the best advice you can, and then move on to more positive things.

If they confide in you that one of their children or another member of their family is doing some hurtful things, don't add your thoughts of how bad they are acting. Remember that even though they are unburdening their heart to you, these people they are talking about are very precious to them, so tread softly with any remarks you make. Praying with them over this situation will comfort them greatly, letting them know that you really care. Then, make sure you don't pass this information along to anyone else. Isn't this how you would want to be treated?

Be in a good mood, whether you feel like it or not, happiness is a choice. It will make everyone uncomfortable to be in your home if someone is angry or upset. Of course, there are times in our life when we are having problems or grieving, but as a rule try to be as kind and loving to everyone as you can be.

It's important to plan ahead so you're not caught off-guard. There may be times when you get a call, and an unexpected guest is going to stop by. If you keep up with your housework, there won't be any major things that need to be done before they arrive. If there is a bit of disorganization, just get a box or laundry basket and go around the house picking up everything that is out of place, and then put the whole container in a closet and out of sight. If you have ironing piled up on the dryer, just put it inside. You can easily take it back out later. It's also good to have a meal in the freezer, like a pan of lasagna or some other yummy casserole, some garlic bread, and a frozen pie or dessert. You can quickly put the lasagna and pie in the oven and they can bake while you greet your guest and visit with them for a while. Then, all you have to do is put some garlic bread in the oven for a few minutes, make a salad, and you will have a very nice meal put together to serve them with very little effort, all because you planned ahead. It's also a good idea to keep some snacks on hand like some chips and dip or cheese and crackers for a quick appetizer while your meal is baking. If you keep these things on hand, you won't be frantically wondering what to do when you get the call that someone is coming.

If you know in advance that guests are coming, it would be wise to do as much work for the meals as you can ahead of time. This will save you a lot of time in the kitchen. Decide on your menu in every detail for each meal you'll be serving. Then, do as much prep work as you can a day or two ahead. Most side dishes can be made and put in the refrigerator, waiting to be cooked or baked when you need them. For breakfast, I often make up my mixes for pancakes or waffles ahead of time. I mix the dry ingredients in one covered container and the wet ingredients in another and put it in the refrigerator. Then, all I have to do in the morning is put the two together and breakfast is ready in a flash. I also may mix up a big batch of scrambled eggs and keep them in the refrigerator the day before and ready to fry up the next morning.

Another wise thing to do is to put together a few different outfits, including accessories. You can put each outfit together on a hanger, choosing from slacks, blouses, dresses, or a sweater or jacket. Then hang a matching necklace or scarf over the hanger and you'll be ready to go anywhere without any hassle.

The key is to plan ahead. This will save you a lot of time, and you will be more confident and comfortable when your guests arrive. All of this will make the visit much more enjoyable for you and for your guests.

Think of how you would like to be treated when you're in someone else's home, and this will tell you just what to do. Wouldn't you like to feel like you are important enough to that person that they would go out of their way to see that you were comfortable and well taken care of?

A Few Words about Being a House Guest

It's always a good idea to bring a little hostess gift, like a jar of your special raspberry jam, or a book you think they would enjoy. Maybe even some special cheese and sausage for the man of the house. It doesn't have to be anything elaborate, just a little "thank you for inviting me" gift.

Be a gracious guest; always be courteous and well mannered. Let them know when you're coming and how long you're going to stay. Don't arrive a lot earlier than they are expecting you, or they may not quite be ready. Also, don't arrive later than you said without calling to let them know you've been delayed.

If you plan to go somewhere else while you're visiting them, tell your host ahead of time so they can make plans accordingly.

As best you can, fit into their schedule. If they eat or go to bed at a certain time you are not accustomed to, don't make an issue out of it, just go along with their schedule. Don't stay up after your hosts go to bed or get up and make noise before they are up. If you do get up first, be considerate and make as little noise as possible. This might be a good time to catch up on your reading.

Take care of your own children; don't expect your hosts to be a babysitter while you are doing other things. If you do need a babysitter, hire one. Maybe one of your host's older children would do it for you. If so, be sure to pay them well.

As much as possible keep your things in your suitcase not strewn about all over the room, and definitely not in other areas of their house.

Pick up and clean up after yourself and your family. Never leave a mess for someone else to clean up. If you are working on a project, as soon as you are finished put things away. This is only common courtesy.

Be careful to turn off the lights in your bedroom or any other room when you leave it if no one else is there.

If you have your own bathroom, ask what towels you are to use, and keep the bathroom clean and picked up. After you shower, hang your wet towels up to dry.

If there is only one bathroom in the house, ask your hosts when would be the best time for you and your family to take showers. Don't take long showers and use all the hot water up or monopolize the bathroom for long periods of time. Always wipe up any water that splatters on or around the sink and countertop. When you leave the bathroom, check to make sure you don't leave any hair in the sink or on the floor and that the commode is clean when you are done using it. If the tissue runs out, put a new roll in the dispenser. Ask where to put your wet towels.

Unless you are told to help yourself, don't assume everything in the refrigerator is free for the taking. Ask and say thank you for anything you are offered. It would no doubt be wise to bring along some snacks like granola bars just in case you need them.

If you are staying more than just overnight, it is a good idea to contribute some groceries, and if your stay is for an extended time, offering some money for the electric bill is a good idea. With more people in the house, utility bills do go up. Even if they don't accept any money, it's good to at least offer or think of another way to repay them.

Help your hostess with meal preparation or setting the table, but don't try to outshine her with your great recipes or stories. Remember, this is her home, and she is the queen of this castle. Offer to clean up the kitchen and load the dishwasher after the meal. Offer to take out the garbage or anything else that needs to be done.

I learned this lesson the hard way. Many years ago, when our children were young, we sometimes spent the weekend at some of our extended family's home. With our family there I thought it was important for me to help cook the meals. Often the lady of the house seemed solemn and out of sorts, and I just couldn't figure out what was going on. I kept wondering if I had said or done something that had upset her. One day I mentioned this to a friend, and she asked me two questions. "Were you making any special dishes as part of the meals, and were people telling you how much they liked them?" I said, "yes" to both questions and then added "but with all of us there isn't it only right to do my part? I didn't want to make this woman do all the work for my family." My friend wisely said, "I think what is happening is that you are getting more praise for your cooking than she is for hers. After all, this is her home." That was a real eye opener for me. From then on, I made sure to do more of the behind-the-scenes things like peeling the potatoes or mashing them, setting the table and washing the dishes afterwards, and to my surprise, the problem was solved.

When you are ready to go home, ask if you can put fresh linens on the bed. Make sure the bathroom is clean, wipe out the sink and empty the trash container. Put a clean hand towel out and put the towels that you have used by the laundry.

Since you want to be invited back, make this visit a good one. It's best not to overstay your welcome. Remember, it's better to leave with them wanting you to stay, than to stay with them wanting you to leave. Leave a small note of appreciation when you leave, or send a thank you card to show you appreciated all that was done for you.

Luke 6:31 instructs us to, *Do to others as you would have them do to you.* If you just think of how you would want a guest to act in your home and do the same when you're a guest in theirs, you'll know just what to do.

Chapter 5

The House

*Commit to the Lord whatever you do
and he will establish your plans.*
Proverbs 16:3

*She watches over the affairs of her household
And does not eat the bread of idleness.*
Proverbs 31:27

In this chapter we will be talking about taking care of the home that God has given us. I will be sharing with you the plans I have made for my own home. I have been using these plans for many years, and they work very well for me. If you choose to try them, I think you will be amazed at how well they will work for you too. Take these plans and modify them to fit your own family and lifestyle, then you'll see the beauty of them for yourself.

Let's start with a silly little story of how Tidy Tilly and Messy Millie start their day. I have to admit that I have identified a bit with both of these little ladies at one time or another.

Tidy Tilly opened her eyes to a new day. She was well rested since she went to bed a little early last night. As she reached to turn the alarm clock off, a few minutes before it was set to ring, she whispered a prayer of thanks for the new day and a good night's sleep. Upon rising, she quickly made her bed and went in to have her morning shower. After she showered, she put her dirty laundry in the hamper and quickly dressed in the clothes she had pressed and laid out the night before, then she went into the kitchen to fix breakfast. Looking at her weekly menu that was taped on the inside of the cupboard door, she saw that scrambled eggs, bacon, and toast were planned for this morning's breakfast. Since she had made her grocery list off her menu she had all the ingredients that she needed. While the bacon and eggs were frying, she set the table and called her family. Then, going to the refrigerator, she took out her children's lunches that she had packed the previous evening. Next, she put them in color-coded bags so each child got the right one and placed them on the counter next to the back door. As she sat his breakfast on the table, six-year-old Bobby said with a smile, "Mmm this breakfast smells good, Mom," then he started gobbling it up. When the family finished their breakfast, each one put their dishes in the dishwasher and went off to finish getting ready for the day ahead. With hugs and waves the children left for school. Tilly's husband gave her a quick kiss on the cheek and said, "Have a good day, honey." As Tilly waved goodbye to her family, she noticed that she had a little extra time before she was due at work. "Maybe I'll stop and pick up a few flowers to put on my desk," she thought with a smile.

Meanwhile, next door at Messy Millie's house, the snooze alarm was going off for the third time. Millie reached over to shut it off one last time, and then struggled to get up. She hadn't slept well last night. She had watched TV until about midnight, and now she was paying for it. She hated being rushed, but this morning she just couldn't get herself going. As she went to her closet, she wondered what she was going to wear. This always seemed to be the question of the day. She took out her favorite green blouse, then remembering that the matching skirt was at the cleaners, she hung it back up. At last, she decided on her old faithful navy-blue skirt, "Oh no," she thought, "my matching blouse is in the dryer", so she quickly went down stairs to the laundry room to get it. When she removed the blouse from the dryer, she saw that it was full of wrinkles, thinking to herself, "Well, maybe it won't look too bad after I wear it a while. Don't they say wrinkles fall out with a little wear?" She quickly put the blouse on and started to button it up only to see that the middle button had fallen off in the dryer. She told herself that if she pinned it together and kept her jacket on all day, no one would even notice. With that she hurried back up the stairs to get breakfast started. She thought some scrambled eggs would be nice, but as she opened the refrigerator door she remembered she had used the last eggs yesterday. "Plan B, cereal will have to do," she told herself. She hurriedly took the boxes down from the cabinet and put them on the table then went to get some bowls. "Can you believe it?" she moaned in exasperation as she realized she had forgotten to start the dishwasher last night. She grabbed a few bowls out of the dishwasher and quickly washed them as the family came to the table for breakfast. "Mom, I didn't have any clean socks. What am I supposed to do, go barefoot?" asked her son Tyler. Millie was placing the last bowl on the table when her daughter came into the kitchen,

"Not cereal again!" she whined, "I wanted scrambled eggs, you know I hate cereal!"

"Well, we're all out of eggs so you're just going to have to eat cereal!" Millie snapped as she futilely searched for something to pack her children's lunch with. Just then, her husband stormed into the kitchen. "Not one decent clean shirt again, I'm trying to make a good impression on my boss, and all I have to wear is this old shirt! I'll grab a doughnut on my way to work," he growled, slamming the door behind him.

With this, Millie slumped into a chair and put her face down into her hands. "There has to be a better way," she sighed, "there just has to be."

This little tale may be a bit exaggerated, well maybe, extremely exaggerated in both directions, but I'm sure you get the point. It shows that creating a plan and carrying out that plan makes all the difference.

Make a System, Plan Ahead

> A home is like a business.
> What would happen to a business,
> without planning ahead?

If we make a plan for every aspect of our home and family and carry out those plans, we will be in control of the events of the day. If we don't, events of the day will control us, and we will constantly be struggling to keep our head above water, so to say. There are so many things in life that no one can do for us; we have to roll up our sleeves, put determination in our hearts, and do what is necessary for ourselves. Once we make a plan and consistently carry it out, we will reap the reward of our efforts.

In Galatians 6:7 the Bible speaks of sowing and reaping. It says, *A man reaps what he sows*. We usually think this scripture only applies to spiritual things, but this also applies to other things in life like taking care of the family and home that God has given us. If we are willing to sow the actions needed to keep our family and home well taken care of, we will reap a happy healthy family, and a beautiful home where peace prevails.

Making a list and planning ahead saves a lot of time in the long run. Writing things down will free our mind from the constant job of trying to remember everything we have to do, and we won't be forgetting important things that need to be done or appointments that have to be kept.

Take control. The word *take* is an action word, and it means we are doing what is necessary in a certain situation and putting forth the effort needed to accomplish a task. Once we have taken the time to put a plan in place and follow that plan, our life will go much smoother. There will be very few times of stress when we have to scurry around to get things done, and surprise guests won't be nearly so overwhelming.

A good thing to help you create a plan and keep it organized is a three-ring notebook. Here you'll be able to keep all your household information. You can add dividers and label them for different sections. Have a space for your menus and a space for family birthdays and anniversaries. In this space list each member of each family you send gifts or cards to. Also list the address and the likes and dislikes of each one. When it is time for a card, gift or a visit, it will be much easier to get something they will really like, and something that shows you are truly thinking of them. Also, have a section for your housework schedule and the information on the periodic maintenance of your household appliances, furnace, and air conditioner.

Another time saver is to set aside a bit of time at the end of each month to get any birthday or anniversary cards for the next month addressed and ready to mail. Write the date of their birthday or anniversary in the top right corner of the envelope where the stamp will go. This will help you make sure you mail them on time and the date will be covered with a stamp. I keep a monthly calendar taped inside the cupboard door that opens up to my dishes. There I list all the birthdays, anniversaries, and appointments for the month ahead so I can see them at a glance.

All of life is made up of choices. We must choose to create consistent habits of organization for our home. There will be times we may not feel like cooking or cleaning, but that doesn't mean we shouldn't do it. God gave us our home and our precious family. That is His part, taking care of them both is our part. The more we do what we know we need to do for our family and home, the easier it will become. Very soon we'll see that our homes are in order and healthy nutritious meals are prepared and served on time. This is another thing that will help bring peace and harmony to our homes.

Procrastination will shipwreck good intentions every time. Diligence will bring success, and we will look around at our clean, organized home with pride knowing that we have taken the necessary steps to be in control. Soon these habits will become automatic and we'll be doing them without even thinking about them.

This will set an example for our children. In school, they will learn the value of diligence in doing their best on their homework and turning it in on time. As they grow older, it will set the pattern they will follow for their own families. As I look back at my dear mother, who was an excellent homemaker, and also at my grandmother who also was an excellent homemaker, I can see where their example has molded my life and embedded in me a desire to follow in their footsteps to be a good homemaker too.

Creating a Home of Peace and Beauty

It is important to spend our time creating a loving, comfortable home for our families, remembering that this is the only safe shelter they have in this buffeting world. So we must do everything we can to make our home a peaceful, happy place to be, and a place of refuge where our family feels safe and secure.

Psalm 34:14 tells us, *Seek peace and pursue it*. Seek and pursue are two very strong action words. They tell us that although peace is possible, it doesn't come without some definite effort on our part. If we want peace we have to do what is necessary to get it. Life can be good and peace can fill our homes if we sincerely make an effort to create it. Creating a peaceful home doesn't happen all by itself. It requires purposeful actions and choices. There are things we will have to start doing and others we will have to stop doing.

Making a habit to stay calm and speak in a calm voice, will go a long way toward bringing peace to our home. Also, playing soft, peaceful, uplifting music will help to create a peaceful atmosphere. Just think of the times you've gone to the mall and overly loud music was playing in a store. If you're anything like me, you just can't wait to get out of there. On the other hand, soft soothing music draws you in and makes you want to stay and browse. Our home should be a peaceful place where our family feels loved and accepted.

The music that is played and the movies that are watched in our home can make a tremendous impression on our children. There was a time when our children were small that the music we played in our home taught us a real lesson. At that time our little boy was just five years old and it was almost Christmas. There was a song that played quite often on the radio that was called "If we make it through December." It talked of a dad who had lost his job in the factory at Christmas time, which meant there would be no Christmas presents for his little girl. The song said over and over the phrase "If we make it through December, everything will be all right." Knowing we worked in a factory and that it was almost Christmas, our little son took this song to heart. One day he came to his father and said with questioning eyes, "We're going to make it through December, aren't we Dad?" At first we reassured him that we were not going to lose our jobs and that Christmas was going to be just fine, thinking this was just something rather cute. But then the reality struck us of the fearful impression the lyrics of this song had made on the mind of our little son. We have to constantly be aware of what is being fed into the mind of our children.

Decorate with a Godly Purpose

Of course we want to make our homes look good, but have you ever considered the fact that how your home is decorated has a big influence on your family? The pictures and sayings that you have on the walls and placed around your home have an enormous and lasting influence on your family, so choose carefully. Remember the arrows we talked about in the "Children of the House" chapter? Here is another way to direct our arrows, which are our children, in the way that they should go.

It's important to choose uplifting pictures and plaques with scriptures on them and also those with uplifting, encouraging words of wisdom to place where the whole family can see and be influenced by them. Deuteronomy 11:19-20 tells us of some instructions and a reward from God. It says, *Teach them* [the commandments of the Lord] *to your children, talking about them when you sit at home and when you walk along the road, when you lie down and when you get up. Write them on the door frames of your houses and on your gates, so that your days and the days of your children may be many in the land the Lord swore to give your ancestors, as many as the days that the heavens are above the earth."* Change these from time to time for when we see the same thing for a long time it no longer makes an impression on us.

A home that is loved by the homemaker not only shows that it is loved, it also radiates love and peace to those who live there. Your family may not recognize it at the time, but when the children are grown and look back on the home of their childhood, they will clearly see all the love and work that was poured into making it a loving and peaceful home for them, and it will make them want to do the same thing for their children.

Clutter

When clutter comes in, peace goes out.

Does our home comfort and make our families feel safe and secure, or does just being there bring stress? Our home should be the one place in the world where there is peace, and we are free from stress. When our home is full of clutter it gives a feeling of chaos and turmoil where all we want to do is escape. On the other hand, when our home is neat and clean it creates a feeling of peace and tranquility, making us content and relaxed, giving us a desire to stay in our cozy home.

Actually, clutter is almost a living thing. By this I mean when we see papers, clothes, toys, or other things out of out of place and lying around, it seems much easier for each member of the family to add to it by leaving even more things lying around where they don't belong. As it starts to grow, it attracts more and more clutter. If this is not kept in check it can end up being the normal way for our home to look. But with the clutter will also come an uneasy, restless feeling that we just can't seem to shake.

Here are some things that too much clutter will do.

It will *steal our time* because we won't be able to find the things we need, and we will spend a lot of time looking for them. They may be right in front of us, but they'll be hidden by so many other things around them we will easily overlook them.

It will *steal our money* because when we need a certain thing but can't find it, even though we know we have it somewhere, in exasperation we will end up going out and buying the same thing again. Also, bills that are due may very well get lost in the pile of papers we have on our desks, and then we will end up having to pay late charges when we do find them.

It will *cause us stress* because each room that we go in will remind us of the work that needs to be done there. It will be like a thought that keeps tormenting us saying, "I have to clean this up, I have to clean this up!" But I just don't have time right now. Also, there will be no place to start a cleaning project because every area is filled, and if we move what is there, where will we put it? Add that to the stress it causes because there is no place to set anything down, not even ourselves. It has been proven many times that stress is one of the major causes of many diseases.

It will also *cause stress among our family members* because each one will think that the other person moved the very thing we are looking for. When we can't find something, we may blame one of our children or our husband. "Where did *you* put my ____?"

It *causes illness* because of the dust it collects, which adds to breathing problems, especially for people with allergies, asthma, COPD, and many other respiratory diseases.

Now that we've looked at the problem, let's take a look at the solution.

The good news is this is a problem that can be solved. When you find clutter piling up, it may be a bit daunting to think you have to take care of it all at one time. But taking one section at a time, even making some small progress, will motivate you to get the rest taken care of. It will take some time and determination, but *you can do it*. Just roll up your sleeves and take one room or even one closet at a time. Get rid of as much as possible. Don't expect to do it all in one day. It took a while to accumulate, and it may take a while to sift through and clean it out. Keep in mind that the more you have, the more you have to take care of and the more room you need to put it.

Once again, remembering the story of "The Little Engine That Could", at first he thought the job was too hard for him, but once he got started he found that he could do far more than he thought he could. Say like he did, "I think I can, I think I can, I think I can," and pretty soon you'll find that you'll know you can! Declutter your own things first, then enlist your family to do theirs.

Ok, let's get started decluttering. Get two boxes. One is for things you want to keep but don't use very often; these you can put somewhere out of the way. The other box is for things you want to give away or donate. There will also be some things you just choose to throw away. I'm sure you've heard the saying, "Less mess, less stress," and this is very true. Keep only the very best things you have and get rid of the rest. Once you get one room cleaned and organized it will give you a great feeling of accomplishment and even more determination to tackle another room. When the clutter is gone you'll have an enormous feeling of relief. Since you've only kept the very best things you have, you will see your home as beautiful and inviting, and a home you can be proud of.

One more good thing to keep in mind is if you have fewer things in a room it will not only make the room look bigger, it will also be easier to keep neat and clean, giving you a sense of peace. Getting rid of clutter will Eliminate a great deal of the housework in our homes. That fact alone should motivate us.

Organized Cleaning

When I was in my early years of homemaking, I lived by an older woman who gave me some good advice as far as ways of cleaning the house. I visited her only a few times and now, so many years later, I realize that I could have learned so much from her had I taken the time to develop a friendship with her. She told me two things that I've done faithfully over the years.

One is, "when you're dusting a room, the horizontal surfaces of anything catch the most dust, so when you're dusting, make a habit to dust all the flat surfaces and don't forget the windowsills." This means that the scroll work that dresses up our furniture is a big dust collector. The other thing she told me was to "regularly wash the inside, top and sides of the dishwasher door, for a lot of things can end up there." A few years later another older lady asked my husband and me over for dinner and as we two ladies were cleaning up after the meal she said, "When you finish with the dishes, always scour out your sink. This does four things: it cleans and disinfects your sink, and it cleans and disinfects your dish cloth, all at the same time." Also good advice that I've practiced over the years.

A major part of keeping a home neat is just a matter of putting things where they belong instead of just putting them down right where they are when you finish using them. After working in any area, always put things away and clean the space where you were working. Teach your children to do this too. This will help keep your home neat and clean. When you're leaving a room make a habit of taking a look around to see if there is anything you've forgotten to pick up and put away.

> Being organized will save lots of steps.
> This is a big-time saver in any job.

If you're going upstairs, ask yourself, "What needs to go up and be put away?" If you're going downstairs, ask yourself, "What needs to go down and be put away?" I often put things at the top or the bottom of the stairs to put away when I'm either going up or down for some other reason. This saves a lot of unnecessary steps. Train yourself to think ahead and make each movement count so you won't have to do a lot of unnecessary backtracking.

For many years I worked in a factory on the assembly line. This is how I got interested in time study. Time study is just a way of trying to get the job done and done right in less and less time. You do this by doing the same thing over and over with a bit of variation each time, always trying to find a way to do the job more efficiently and still getting it done with the same degree of excellence.

Over the years, I've used it to work out a home cleaning method that works very well for me. I'm going to share it with you here. Once you get it set up and do it a few times you will find that it works quite well, and you'll get your housework done, and done skillfully, in no time at all. Setting it up does take a bit of time, but you only have to do that once. You'll spend that time gathering everything you'll need and putting them in place. Then, the first time or two that you do it this way, it will take a little longer because you'll be forming new habits. But once you do these things, you'll find that your housework will take less time than you ever thought possible.

Making a List and Checking it Twice

So here we go. Go into every room and make a list of everything that needs to be done once a week. Now remember, we're only talking about our weekly cleaning, not our deep cleaning. Rooms that are used more need to be cleaned more often. There are some rooms that may not need to be cleaned every week. Then, time yourself while you clean each room and record it on a card. There are a few things that need to be done every day like making beds or preparing meals. I don't put these on my cleaning list.

Keep your deep cleaning schedule in your three-ringed notebook. This consists of the cleaning that needs to be done monthly, bi-monthly, every six months, and the yearly cleaning.

Divide up all your weekly jobs so that you have similar times to complete them and then spread your cleaning out over the five days of the week or however many days will work for your schedule. I have done mine different ways depending on how much time I had to allot for cleaning. At one time I spread it out over five days, then for a while I did it all in three days, and at other times I've cleaned one room a day and when I had all the rooms finished, I started all over again. You will know what fits your home and lifestyle.

Once you get this cleaning schedule in place and you have practiced it a few times, you'll realize that working straight through each room without stopping will have you finished cleaning in no time at all. A whole room that is completely cleaned will give you a greater sense of accomplishment than you would have if you did just a bit of cleaning here and there throughout your home.

A lot of times you will find that something you have on your cleaning list really doesn't need as much attention as usual. Maybe just a spot cleaning will do the job just as well. If it isn't dirty or dusty, don't waste your time cleaning it, move on to the next thing on your list.

Be realistic, and don't add unnecessary work. The whole house doesn't need to be dusted every day, some of it may not even need to be dusted every week. There are times we sabotage ourselves.

As you look over your list, you'll find that a lot of things don't have to be done by you. Never, ever forget that a lot of these jobs can and should be delegated to other members of your family. We do our family a disservice if we do everything that needs to be done ourselves. In their mind we will have planted the idea that they are not responsible for any of the day-to-day household chores. Everyone who lives in the home should be taught that each one of them is responsible to help keep the house neat and clean. Even small children can do something that fits their ability. Make this a team effort. The other thing this does is train them how to do household jobs so when they grow up and get a home of their own, they will already know how to take good care of it.

If your little one wants you to read a story to them while you're doing your housework. See if there is something they can do to help you, so they don't feel neglected. Ask them to throw away the garbage you've collected or help you do something. Including them in what you're doing will give them the feeling of closeness, and that is really what they want. Children should never feel like they are less important than our housework. After all, we're doing all this for our precious family.

Keeping a list of what you need to do helps you say no when a friend wants to include you in their plans for the day. You can just politely say, "I'm sorry, but I already have plans for today, maybe next time." Remember, your family and your home come before your friends on your priority list.

Make your schedule and keep to it as much as possible, but don't be too rigid. There are times when we have to put our schedule aside for something that is more important.

Learn the difference between needless interruptions, and those that are worth taking time out for. But make putting your schedule aside the exception, not the rule.

I may sound like I'm contradicting myself here, but we always need to remember that balance is the key. Being too rigid is not good for anyone, but neither is repeated procrastination. With that in mind, don't insist on a home that is always spotless, this makes it uncomfortable for our family or those who visit us. We've all heard of husbands who say they stay out in the garage because they are uncomfortable in their own home. Don't let this happen to your husband.

I once had an experience with this that opened my eyes. At that time, my parents lived about four hundred miles away from us so we didn't get to see them very often. Whenever they came, I would work myself into a frenzy trying get everything perfect and wanting to make a good impression on them. That was until my mother came to me and said that she was afraid to wash her hands in the bathroom sink because it was so clean she thought she might leave some water spots on it. This made us both feel bad. Yes, indeed, balances is the key.

We can so easily get caught up in all the demands of work that needs to be done around the house, that without realizing it we can neglect spending time with our precious family. Remember, we're doing all this planning and organizing so that our work around the house will take less time and make more time to spend with our family. Cherish the years your children are home with you, they are precious years, and they are gone all too soon.

Ok, Now we're going to look at getting our home cleaning plan in place. Remember, as I've said before, this plan takes more time initially to get set up than it does to actually do, and you only have to do this once.

Products and Tools That You Will Need

Cleaning products:
Furniture Polish
Glass cleaner
409 cleaner or my own personal cleaner *
Comet cleanser
Toilet bowl cleaner
Disinfectant spray
Floor cleaner (try to find one with a pleasant fragrance)

Cleaning tools:
A cleaning caddy with a handle
2 small different-colored spray bottles
    1 for general cleaning, 409
    1 for glass cleaner
Another small bottle to keep floor cleaner in
A sponge with a scratcher on the back of it
Folded pieces of paper towel
Soft cleaning cloths
Micro-fiber cleaning cloths **
    You'll be using these to dust with, and also to put on your Swiffer Sweeper, if you have one
2 different colored toothbrushes

1 for cleaning around faucets, light switches or any small, hard to get to places.

1 for cleaning toilet seat hinges and the base of the toilet. Rinse this toothbrush in a disinfectant when you are finished using it, and keep it in a small zip bag so if there are any germs left on it, they won't get on anything else.

Toilet bowl brush
1 long-handled dust wand
A Swiffer Sweeper or a dust mop
A broom and dustpan
A vacuum
A mop and a pail

When it comes to mopping, I use a spray mop. It's one that has a cartridge with floor cleaner in it and it also has a trigger on the handle that sprays the floor cleaner as needed. It has a pad that is held on by Velcro for wiping up the floor. The pad is washable, and the cartridge is refillable. This mop cleans the floor beautifully and really cuts down on the time it takes to get the job done.

A friend gave me this recipe for an excellent cleaner that you may want to try, and it works great on any greasy surfaces or in the shower to remove the soap film on the shower walls.

*My all-purpose cleaner
   In a quart spray bottle, pour,
   1/4 cup dark blue Dawn dish soap
   1/2 cup lemon juice
   1 cup white vinegar
   1 1/4 cup water

**A word about microfiber cloths; I think when it comes to cleaning and dusting, microfiber is one of the greatest inventions ever made. They hold on to the dust and dirt so it doesn't spread around. I've also found a couple of other uses for them. If you have a Swiffer Sweeper, you can put a microfiber cloth on it just like you would a new Swiffer cleaning cloth. It works great to use on your floors for cleaning up dust and dirt. The only difference is that once you've used it you don't have to throw it away and buy a new one. You just wash them, and use them over and over again. I also put one on my long-handled dust wand. I fold it over the end of it and wrap a rubber band around it to hold it in place. This is great for reaching up high to knock down cobwebs and no more crawling along the floor to dust the base boards. Just walk along with your duster wiping as you go. Make sure when you're done to always take the micro-fiber cloth off folding it into itself so the dust and dirt are trapped inside. Then shake it out into the garbage can and put it in the hamper to be washed with the laundry. These wash up beautifully and last through untold times of washing.

Organizing the Cleaning Caddy

When you get ready to start the cleaning project, start by organizing everything you will need for the job that you are going to do.

I use a cleaning caddy with a handle for easy carrying. It works very well to keep all the cleaners and cleaning cloths in. If you don't have one, a pail will also carry all the cleaning supplies in it. Use as many products as you can that can do double duty instead of a different product for each thing. For example, Windex not only works great for cleaning windows and mirrors but also for counter tops and even for some spot cleaning. The benefit of using fewer items is that you'll have less to carry around, making that part of your job easier. Something else that will help is using smaller containers for some of your cleaners. You won't need the whole bottle of Windex, 409 or floor cleaner for the cleaning you are doing today. Pouring some into smaller bottles will make more room in your cleaning caddy, and it won't be as heavy to carry. Just remember, when you finish the cleaning project to refill each of the smaller bottles so you're ready to go the next time you need them.

Since you're only using your disinfectant spray, toilet bowl cleaner, and brush in the bathroom, leave them there in an easily accessible place. There's no need to haul them around from room to room.

Put your cleaning products and sponge in one side of the cleaning caddy and on the other side use half for your folded microfiber, soft cloths, and folded pieces of paper towel. Use the other half to fit in a little plastic bag or container to put your soiled cloths and wet paper towels in. Make sure you also have a place for your toothbrushes.

When you start a room, find a central spot to place the cleaning caddy that can be easily reached from anywhere in the room. Always put each cleaning item back in the same place in the cleaning caddy, this will make it much easier to get what you need at a glance, the next time you need it.

Move around the room cleaning from one side to the other so you don't have to backtrack. Begin inside the door with your long-handled duster checking for cobwebs and then cleaning and dusting the cabinet all the way to the floor, top to bottom. The top cabinets will most likely be clean of dirt or any marks; these are usually the ones that we should check in our bi-weekly or monthly cleaning routine. Then, proceed all the way continuously around the room, cleaning cabinets, windows, mirrors, and everything as you go. Always keeping in mind that horizontal surfaces collect more dirt and dust than vertical ones do.

Finally, sweep, Swiffer, mop, or vacuum the floor, which ever one is needed. The floor should always be the last thing cleaned in the room because dust and dirt will naturally fall on it while we're cleaning the rest of the room.

Ok let's start cleaning!

Kitchen

First, take a basket or box and put everything that does not belong here in it to be put away later, then straighten and put away everything else that needs it.

I usually find that of all the rooms we have in our homes, the kitchen takes the longest time to clean. The reason is that the kitchen seems to get a build-up of grease almost everywhere from day-to-day cooking, especially on, above, and below the stove, and also on the cabinets that are closest to it. Another reason is because the kitchen has so many cabinets and appliances to clean, that these things make it quite time consuming.

Keep as few things as possible on your kitchen counters. This will make cleaning your kitchen much easier and give you more space to work.

Start cleaning just inside the door and clean from top to bottom, then from one side to the other, all the way around the room. You'll probably start with your high kitchen cupboards. These are usually ok, but you may find some fingerprints around the door handles that need to be cleaned. Check the inside of the door too.

Remember, if it isn't dirty, move on to the next thing. If it is dirty, take your 409 and give it a spray, then wipe it off. Hold the spray bottle in one hand and your soft cleaning cloth in the other, this will make for fast work, as you work your way around the room. Unless it's needed, don't spray the whole cabinet.

Next, starting in the back of your counter, pull everything forward and spray and wipe the area where they were. Then, take everything that is on the counter and check each one to see if they need a quick wipe, and put them back in place. This is when you will be thankful you don't have a lot of unnecessary knick-knacks and small appliances on your counter. Now, spray and wipe the rest of your counter, then check the bottom cupboards and spray and wipe as needed. Always wipe the top ledge of drawers and cabinet doors as you come to them and check around the handle and the handle itself. You may need to use your toothbrush if the handles have any gunk around them. When you get to your sink, get it wet and sprinkle your cleanser in it. Wipe it down and give it a good rinse, then clean and shine the faucet. Now, clean the counters and cabinets on the other side of the sink as you did the first. Wipe down the refrigerator, stove, dishwasher, and microwave as needed when you come to them.

When you come to your windows, take your glass cleaner and a paper towel to clean them if they need to be washed. They too may just need a spot cleaning. When you're washing a window or mirror, stand off to the side when checking it for streaks. You'll be able to see them far better that way.

Clean the floor last. When mopping the floor, if you've done a lot of frying, start by spraying some 409 on the floor in front of the stove so it can start dissolving any grease that has splattered there.

Living Room

First, take a basket or box and put everything that does not belong here in it to be put away later, then straighten and put away everything else that needs it.

As you do in every room, start inside the door cleaning as you go from top to bottom, and from one side of the room to the other, all the way around. Don't forget the top of picture frames and the windowsills, remembering that flat surfaces collect more dust than vertical ones do. Wash the windows and mirrors as needed, as you go. Picture frames with glass usually only need to be dusted, but occasionally you will need to wash the glass.

Now that the perimeter of the room is done, dust the lampshades and lamps, then dust and polish the end tables and coffee table. If anything on them needs to be cleaned, do that at this time. With a microfiber cloth, wipe the TV screen, then wipe the back and sides of the TV.

Next, vacuum or dust the couch, couch pillows, and chairs, depending on the material they are made of. Don't forget to remove the cushions on the couch and vacuum under each one as needed. Use your toothbrush to clean around any buttons or piping they may have if they need it.

Clean the floor last.

Bedroom

First, take a basket or box and put everything that does not belong here in it to be put away later, then straighten and put away everything else that needs it.

Start inside the door, cleaning from top to bottom and from one side to the other, all the way around the room as you do in every room. Dust everything. Don't forget the top of picture frames and the windowsills, remembering that flat surfaces collect more dust than vertical ones do, washing windows and mirrors as you go. Remember, if it doesn't need to be cleaned, move on to the next thing on your list.

Dust and polish the headboard of the bed, the dresser, chest of drawers' top, front, and sides, and also the nightstands, as needed. Wipe down the lamp shades and lamps and any knick-knacks as needed also.

Clean the floor last. If your floors are hardwood or vinyl, sweep or dustmop them weekly and damp mop them monthly. If they are carpeted, they should be vacuumed weekly or as needed.

Sheets should be washed once a week in hot water. Three or four times a year wash the pillows, blankets, and the mattress cover. Vacuum the mattress once a month.

Since we spend a third of our life sleeping, we should keep our beds and bedrooms as dust free as possible.

When a family member is sick, their bedding should be washed in hot water as often as needed to keep germs from spreading, especially the sheets and pillowcases. Use either bleach or color safe bleach to disinfect them.

Bathroom

First, take a basket or box and put everything that does not belong here in it to be put away later, then straighten and put away everything else that needs it.

The next thing to do in the bathroom is to get the toilet bowl cleaner and spray some all around the inside of the toilet bowl. Don't forget to spray some under the rim. Next get the shower wet and then spray the shower down with your shower cleaner, top to bottom, walls and tub.

Then, start as usual inside the door, cleaning from top to bottom, and from one side to the other all the way around the room. Clean the windows, mirrors, and any cabinets as you go.

When you come to your counter by the sink, put your arms around all the bottles on one side of the sink and pull them forward, spray and wipe where they were, then take each one and wipe it off including the bottom, as needed, and put it back in place. Get the sink wet, then sprinkle some of the cleanser in it and wipe it down. Next, give it a good rinse then clean and shine the faucet. After that, clean the other side of the counter the same as the first. Check the cabinets below and spray and wipe as needed.

The shower should still be wet, so use your sponge to scrub it down, then rinse it. You may have to use the back side of the sponge that has the scratcher on it if you have a soap buildup on the shower walls. If you do this regularly you will find that it cleans easier each time. Sprinkle some cleanser on the floor of the shower, give it a good scrub, and then rinse it. If there is a soap build up on the floor, it can get quite slippery, which can easily cause an accident getting in or out of the tub.

When cleaning the toilet, spray some of your disinfectant spray on the top of the tank, and then on the tank itself before you wipe it clean. Next, spray the seat hinges and then take your toilet toothbrush and clean around them as needed, and wipe them clean. Spray and wipe the lid, top and bottom, and the seat top and bottom, then take the toilet brush and clean the inside of the bowl. Don't forget to scrub under the rim. Lastly, use your disinfectant spray to spray and wipe the outside of the bowl all the way to the floor, then use your toilet toothbrush to clean around the base of the toilet if it needs it. If you have little boys, you may have to clean the toilet area more often.

As usual, clean the floor last.

Laundry Room

First, take a basket or box and put everything that does not belong here in it to be put away later, then straighten and put away everything else that needs it.

Start inside the door cleaning from top to bottom, and from side to side, all the way around the room as you do in every room. As you go, dust everything. Don't forget the top of picture frames and the windowsills, remembering that flat surfaces collect more dust than vertical ones do. If needed, wash windows and mirrors as you go. Remember, if it doesn't need to be cleaned, move on to the next thing on your list.

The outside of the washer and dryer usually only needs a damp cloth run over them to keep them clean. Lift the lid of the washer and spray some 409 around the top of the load basket then wipe and clean it as needed. Also, as needed, clean the inside of the dryer door.

Clean the floor last.

A Few Helpful Hints

Remove lint from the lint screen in the dryer after every load. If this is left to build up it can start a fire.

For a long time my towels didn't smell fresh when I washed them. I could put bleach in the white ones, but the dark-colored towels often had a sour smell. I thought they weren't getting dry enough, so I tried drying them longer, but that didn't help. Finally, I did some research and found, to my happy surprise, that simply adding a cup of white vinegar to the wash water, took the sour smell away, and even worked as a fabric softener.

To keep dark colored clothes from fading, turn them inside out when you put them in the washer. Also, unless these clothes are especially dirty, wash them in cold water with a mild, cold water laundry detergent on the gentle cycle, then air dry them on a laundry rack.

My mother taught me this little trick for removing stains from the laundry; dark blue Dawn dish soap is an excellent spot remover. Here's how we do it. Get the garment wet, put some dish soap on the spot, and then rub it in a bit. Then, just wash it with the rest of the clothes. You'll be amazed how great this works to remove spots and stains. I keep a bottle of it by my washer for easy access.

If you don't use fabric softener when washing white socks, they will stay white longer. The softener puts a film on the socks that makes dirt stick to them.

To remove blood from clothing or any other material, put peroxide on the stain and rinse it in cold water. Sometimes you have to put this on more than once and scrub it a bit, but it will take the stain out.

When you find that you have a ring around the inside of your collar, which is caused from the oils that we have in our skin, a good way to remove it is to get the material wet and put some dark blue Dawn dish soap all along the stain. Let it set for a few minutes to work, and then gently scrub and rinse it.

Organizing the Kitchen

A well-organized kitchen makes the work we do in it go more efficiently, which helps tremendously in food preparation. I have moved many times, and every time I moved, I kept organizing and reorganizing my kitchen, trying to get my design just right until I came up with the plan I am going to share with you here.

You will save a lot of steps every day if you organize your kitchen by putting what you use, where you use it. Also, place things you use the most on easy-to-access shelves, and those used less often on the shelves that are a little more out of the way.

This is how I organize my kitchen.

    Make a drawing of your kitchen. Start on one side and go all the way around the room. Draw a sketch of each cabinet, each drawer, and where the stove, refrigerator, and dishwasher are. Draw where the windows and sink are located. After that, draw a line through each cabinet showing each shelf that is in it. Then number each shelf and each drawer.

    When that is finished, make a list of all your dishes, cups, glasses, bowls, cooking utensils, and flatware. Also, make a list of all the serving dishes, casseroles, pots, pans, and all the small appliances you have. Then, make another list of everything you have in your pantry. Next, it is time to decide where each item will work the best and place the number of the shelf or drawer next to each item on your list. Now it is time to place each item where it belongs. For example, place the coffee, coffee filters, and coffee cup close to the coffee maker. Dishes go in the cabinet close to the dishwasher, and the dishwasher soap goes under the sink and close to the dishwasher.

    Create a cooking station and a baking station. In the cooking station put all of your pots and pans with their covers and the spices you use for cooking close to them. In your baking station put all of your mixing bowls, measuring utensils, pie dishes, cookie sheets, cake and cupcake pans, and all your baking spices close to them.

Meals

It's important to prepare good and nourishing meals for your family. But if it's time to start a meal and you haven't decided what to fix, you may end up just looking for something quick to put together and then you may find that you don't have all the right ingredients. If you are frantically running around the kitchen trying to find something to quickly throw together, you will automatically spread a feeling of tension to other members of your family. This will not be a very pleasant way to share a meal together. Remember that as Psalm 34:14 tells us we must, *seek peace and* [we must] *pursue it.*

Planning a weekly menu for every meal you'll need will save you a lot of time, energy, and money. You will find if you plan ahead, your meal will be easier to make because you'll start knowing that you have already decided what you want to make and how to put it together. It will also be better in nutrition, taste, and presentation with less food wasted. If you plan meals with your family, they'll enjoy helping you make the meals and look forward to eating them. Planning your menu will give you a direction and will ease your mind from the daily dilemma of, "what's for dinner?" Of course, there will be times you choose to switch your daily meals around to fit your taste and schedule.

This is how I create my menus. I make a list of all my family's favorite breakfasts, lunches, and dinners. Then, I make another list of all the side dishes that will go with each one. I also make an additional list of the desserts my family especially likes. Then, I draw from these to fill out my menus for the week or even the month ahead. Once I have my menu planned, I use it to make my grocery list so I have everything on hand that I will need.

By creating a menu and shopping for the things you need, you will save a lot of time since you won't have to stop by the market on the way home from work or get home and then have to run to the market for just a few items. Try to keep a well-stocked pantry, especially the staples of flour, sugar, oil, rice, and canned goods.

Keep your menus on file in your household planner, and then you can draw from these to create new ones. When you make a meal that everyone especially likes, make a note of it on your menu list.

Write down each entrée and what other food you served with the meal that made it a winner for your family. After a while, you'll have a "go to" list of meals that everyone enjoys.

Don't limit yourself to just a few recipes. It's too easy to get a habit of using the same few meals over and over. Add new things from time to time. There is a wealth of recipe sites online these days with excellent recipes that are easy to make. My favorite recipe site is allrecipes.com. There is a multitude of wonderful recipes there, and many reviews on each one.

When making a large meal, look over the menu you've planned. No doubt you'll find that some of the dishes you have planned to make are ok to make a day or two ahead. If so, do that. Also, many things, especially baked goods, can be made and put in the freezer even a week ahead and will stay fresh. Then, just take them out of the freezer the morning of your meal and unwrap and thaw them.

Use your time wisely. While waiting for something that is baking in the oven, use that time to put dishes in the dishwasher or empty it, clean off the counters, straighten a drawer, wiped down the refrigerator, or do a little prep work for the next meal you'll be making. There are many jobs in the kitchen that take only a few minutes and can be done while you wait. Constant vigilance keeps things done.

When you find that you have extra time, another time saver is to take a look at your menus for the week ahead and do any prep work that you can. You can also fix salad like they do on a salad bar. Keep individual items in separate dishes in the refrigerator; they will last a few days like that. Then when it is time for a meal, line up the salad items on the counter and let each one make their own salad. Something I like to do is to keep a pint jar of diced onion and also one of sliced onions in the refrigerator. When making a meal, I find this to be a great time saver too.

To make lettuce last longer, remove the core and wrap it loosely in a damp paper towel and then put it in a plastic bag or container that can be sealed. Small cherry tomatoes will stay fresh longer than a large tomato that is diced.

When using the microwave, if a piece of paper towel is placed over the food, there will be less splatters because the paper towel will catch them. Never put things like plastic containers or cover anything with plastic in the microwave. Have you ever noticed that some plastic containers get blisters on them after being used in the microwave a few times? The microwave will make the plastic melt just enough to let oils in the plastic drip into your food. People have gotten sick from this.

Preparing Meals

After choosing your entrée and all the side dishes for the meal, find the lengthiest total time of preparing and cooking or baking called for in your recipes; this will tell you when to start preparing your meal and how long it will take to prepare it. Some recipes have the total time needed to prepare it listed on the recipe. On the ones that don't, you can time them yourself and write the time it takes to prepare them on the recipe. Then the next time you make that recipe you'll know the total time it takes, from start to finish.

When you start to cook or bake, fill the sink with hot soapy water and put the dirty dishes that don't go in the dishwasher in it when you're done using them. This way you will clean as you go and have the dishes soaking while you finish cooking. This will make for an easy clean up.

When you decide what food you're going to serve, think carefully about how to arrange it on the plate to make it look attractive, and, most of all, appetizing.

People eat better when served food that looks good on their plate. Make your table and each plate of food attractive, remembering we eat first with our eyes. Take note of the plate you're served in a restaurant. See how just a few well-placed items can make a plate of food look more appetizing. Adding a sprig of parsley, a pickle, or a tomato slice on a bed of lettuce will do this for the plate of food you serve. With breakfast, a slice of orange or a couple strawberries perk up a breakfast of eggs and toast. I sometimes take a picture of my restaurant meal or even make a quick sketch of how the food was arranged on the plate and then do the same thing at home.

Serving your meals with lots of smiles will let your family know that you're happy to have them there and you love being there with them.

In our home, we hold hands and pray before each meal. The Bible instructs us to be thankful for everything the Lord provides for us. Doing this not only acknowledges that we realize the Lord provides this food for us, it also tells the Lord how very thankful we are for our food and puts a blessing on it. End your prayer with a smile and a little squeeze for the person's hand that you're holding.

Try to have at least one meal a day where the whole family sits down together. Talk over your day and ask the children about theirs. Ask questions like "did anything special happen today," or "did you have a dream last night?" Children love to tell you stories about their dreams. This will make lasting memories and bind your family close together. Make the dinner table a special place, a place where the whole family enjoys gathering together and enjoying each other's company.

Make a rule that there will be no arguing, just bonding around the table at mealtime. If any correction has to be dealt with, if at all possible, don't do it at the table. Table manners can be taught at other times. Set some time aside to teach the children the correct way to behave at the table. If children are unruly at the table, just separating them and placing one by dad and one by mom often takes care of the problem.

After every meal, the kitchen should be cleaned. The dishes that go in the dishwasher should be put there, and those that don't should be washed, dried, and put away. Everything that was used for making the meal need to be cleaned and put away also. The table, counters, and stove should be washed down, and if it needs it, the floor should be swept.

Make-Ahead Meals

Making a few meals to keep in the freezer will be a tremendous help to you for those days when you have more to do than time to do it. Most of the time spent preparing a meal is the time used to get things assembled and then the cleaning up afterward. It doesn't take a lot of extra time to double your recipe, then you'll have one meal for now, and one to put in the freezer to use later on. This is especially easy to do with casseroles and cookie and pie dough. Put a label on them stating the contents, the date they were made, and the baking instructions. If you do this a time or two a week, you will build up a good supply to use when you need it. It's also good to keep a supply of baked goods in the freezer just in case you need them. The internet holds countless sites where you can find recipes to help you stock your freezer. Make sure you wrap what you put in your freezer really well to ensure your food stays fresh for a long time. I wrap mine in two or three layers of plastic wrap, then in foil, making sure to get as much air out of each layer of wrapping as I can. This way, the food I put in the freezer stays fresh much longer.

Another advantage to putting a few meals in the freezer is that you have a great meal when unexpected guests arrive. All you have to do is take a pan of lasagna or casserole and a dessert out of the freezer and put them in the oven upon their arrival. Then, while you're visiting it will be baking and making your house smell wonderful and homey. Lastly, all you have to do is make a salad and toast some garlic bread and your meal will be done and ready to put on the table.

I was once given a "gift in a jar" as a Christmas present and when I was using it, I thought, "What a great gift idea. Thinking further I thought, "I'll make some of these for myself, using my tried-and-true recipes." I just layer the dry ingredients into a jar and then tape a note on the front of it with the name of the contents, the date, the remaining wet ingredients to add, the oven temperature, and the time it needs to bake.

I did find that if these are stored very long, the moisture in the brown sugar will be absorbed by the other ingredients, leaving the brown sugar hard, so I either put the brown sugar in a small zip bag by itself on the top of the rest of the ingredients, or I add it to my list of things to mix with the wet ingredients.

I have made a lot of mixes this way to keep in the pantry. Not only are they handy to have, but I know exactly what is in each one. I've also found that I can use up to 1/4 less sugar than called for with very little change in the taste of most things.

These make-ahead items can easily be used for a gift for a sick friend or new mom. Just use one of your freezer meals wrapped in a pretty dishtowel and a "dessert in a jar" with a little ribbon or raffia wrapped around the neck of the jar decorating it. These will be greatly appreciated and the recipient can bake them at their own convenience. You can also use these "gift in a jar" items to add to a gift basket for any occasion.

A Few Helpful Hints

Our daughter taught us this little trick. To keep a pan from boiling over, place a wooden spoon across the top of it. When it starts to boil, and it won't boil over.

Keep your dishcloth from staining by using a paper towel or a sponge to clean up things that will stain like coffee, chocolate, and tomato sauce.

Too many suds in the sink when you drain out the water? Cold water will get rid of the suds faster than warm water.

To keep a bowl or pan from moving around while you're mixing what's in it, place a damp cloth under it.

If your brown sugar becomes dry or hard, put it in an airtight container or bag with a slice of bread. The moisture from the bread will transfer to the brown sugar and soften it back up. This works for cookies too.

After frying fish, an easy way to get the smell of fish out of the air is to put two cups of water and one fourth cup of white vinegar in a pan to boil. This will clean the fishy smell out of the air in no time at all. Actually, this works on any bad odor.

If you are going to be handling raw meat, put some warm water with a small amount of bleach in the sink and wash not only your hands but also your countertop or anything that the raw meat has touched. We don't want our families to get sick from any of those nasty germs.

Special Days

Make birthdays special for your family. Have a special plate for the birthday person. Try to find one that says, "Happy Birthday," on it, but if not find one that is extra special to use. Make the birthday person's favorite meal or let them choose a meal. Sing a happy birthday song, and then have your family clap for them. Do their favorite things throughout the day as much as possible. If it's a school day, pack a special lunch for your child with a small gift or surprise tucked inside with a sweet note. All day long make them feel loved and important, excusing them from chores for this one day and pampering them a bit. Tell the children stories of their birth and how you chose their name. This is a story they will never get tired of. Don't forget to give your husband some extra pampering on his birthday too. If he's working that day, send him a little love note. Have your children help you pamper their father; they'll love doing it. A good thing to do would be to have them each think of something special their dad has done for them or something they especially love about him, and then make him a birthday card listing those things. Have them start doing this a few days ahead so they are finished with it on his birthday. Tell them that this is a secret; that will make them enjoy it even more.

On the occasion where the children or your husband has earned special recognition for an outstanding accomplishment, make a special day here too. Make your husband's favorite meal and dessert and tell the children in his presence what he has done that is so special. You may even want your children to clap for Dad. For the children, make their favorite meal and dessert. Let them know that you are proud of them and what they have done. Take a picture of them with their award or a special drawing and post in on the refrigerator, clap for them too. Good grades and good behavior always deserve special recognition.

I once worked with a woman who said she often used her best dishes for her family; you know the ones we usually put away except for special company. Her reason was that her family were the most important people in her life, and she wanted them to know that. I think this is some good advice, don't you?

First Aid

It is good to have your whole family learn some basic first aid. You should also have a first aid kit with the basic supplies in it. Teach each member of your family what to do in case of an accident or emergency, and then they will be prepared ahead of time and they'll know just what to do should this happen. This will keep your family prepared in case of an emergency. Small things we can take care of ourselves, but there are times when we need a doctor, so don't hesitate to see them should that occur.

Keep important phone numbers (911, the local police station) by the phone in an easy place to find for all the family in case of an emergency. For times when your children are home with a babysitter, in a prominent place put the phone number where you can be reached and the phone number of a friend or family member the babysitter can call for help in case they can't get ahold of you.

In Conclusion

I hope the plans I have laid out for you here will help you create a home of peace and love where your family will feel safe and secure, one that radiates the love of Christ. A home that is neat and clean, with wonderful meals made that your family will enjoy. Once you do, you'll never have to be overwhelmed with housework that needs to be done or your meal preparation, because everything will be done in a timely manner and the most you will have to do when you find that unexpected guests are arriving will be to pick up a few stray things.

Printed in the USA
CPSIA information can be obtained
at www.ICGtesting.com
CBHW071458040324
4957CB00007B/177